COACHING THE LITTLE LEAGUE®
PITCHER

TEACHING YOUNG PLAYERS
to Pitch with Skill and Confidence

RANDY VOORHEES

Contemporary Books

Chicago   New York   San Francisco   Lisbon   London   Madrid   Mexico City
Milan   New Delhi   San Juan   Seoul   Singapore   Sydney   Toronto

Library of Congress Cataloging-in-Publication Data

Voorhees, Randy.
     Coaching the Little League pitcher : teaching young players to pitch with skill and confidence / Randy Voorhees.
        p.   cm.
     Includes index.
     ISBN 0-07-140806-1
     1. Pitching (Baseball).   2. Baseball for children—Coaching.   3. Little League baseball.   I. Title.

GV871.V66   2003
796.357'22—dc21   2002041529

3 4 5 6 7 8 9 0 FGR/FGR 2 1 0 9 8 7 6 5 4

ISBN 0-07-140806-1

Interior photographs by Michael Plunkett

McGraw-Hill books are available at special quantity discounts to use as premiums and sales promotions, or for use in corporate training programs. For more information, please write to the Director of Special Sales, Professional Publishing, McGraw-Hill, Two Penn Plaza, New York, NY 10121-2298. Or contact your local bookstore.

This book is printed on acid-free paper.

This book is dedicated to my friend Dave Gallagher, who confesses to knowing little about pitching. He knows plenty, though, about being a man.

Contents

Acknowledgments

I wrote this book because I love teaching baseball pitchers, especially the youngest ones. Many people helped me along the way. To the following people I say, "Thanks":

Rob Taylor, editor at Contemporary Books, for believing in the concept and in me.

Mark Gola, my good friend, for reading the text, supervising the photography, and providing me with a hitter's perspective.

Michael Plunkett, the photographer, for creating the pictures that complement the text.

Dave Gallagher, for believing in me and giving me an opportunity to earn a living doing something that I love.

Joe Carbone, Lou Cioppi, Herman "Champ" Clark, Hank de Simone, Howard "Bubby" Gailloux, Preston "Butch" Miller, and John Monteleone—my baseball coaches from Little League through college.

Gene Palazzi, the president of Hamilton Township Recreational Baseball Association, for allowing use of Van Horn Field for the photography session. Thanks to the entire Hamilton Fire team for modeling for the photographs: Mark Gonzalez Sr. (coach), Rick Storaci Sr. (coach), Colin Cento, Daniel Cifelli Jr., Robert Clausen, Mark Gonzalez Jr., Ryan Inman, Rick McLaughlin, Jim Narmun,

Acknowledgments

Ryan Plunkett, Michael Ridolfino, Rick Storaci Jr., Robert Vanisko, and John Young.

Vince Morgante (Nottingham Little League), for also serving as a model.

Carol and Sarah Voorhees, my wife and daughter, for your patience, understanding, and unwavering support. No man, not even a pitcher, is an island.

Introduction

This book is for anyone who wants to help Little League–age kids become better pitchers. It's for moms, dads, brothers, sisters, aunts, uncles, and the thousands of selfless volunteer coaches who give their time so that kids can have fun playing competitive baseball. The book has eight chapters (nine seemed too contrived) covering topics such as pitching mechanics, individual pitches (fastball, change-up, curveball), strategy and tactics, fielding, and fitness.

The premise of this book is that there is definitely a preferred way—a right way—to pitch a baseball. If kids are taught properly at an early age, they'll perform better and enjoy the game more. Does the art of pitching offer some room for individual style? Yes, of course it does. There are absolutes in pitching, to be sure, but idiosyncrasies are allowed, too.

Pitchers will have different leg lifts, different grips, and different hand positions at release (they'll come in all shapes and sizes, too). That's fine. Just make sure they are natural-born idiosyncrasies, and not something copied from a New York Yankees pitcher just because he cuts an imposing figure in his uniform or because he once agreed to an autograph request. It's great to be a fan, but when it comes to your performance, it's best to be yourself.

Some of this instruction may sound simplistic; that's because it's intended to. In pitching, simple is usually best. As Atlanta Braves pitching coach Leo Mazzone says, "One of the things about pitching is that a lot of people try to make it a lot more complicated than it really is. . . . Why turn something as basic as throwing a baseball into a science project?"

Even though I've tried to be clear and straightforward, some of the instruction may confound or confuse you. If I have failed to make something clear to you, please write to me in care of Mercer County Community College, Trenton, New Jersey 08690, and I'll try to clarify it for you.

Please pay particular attention to the sections on the proper mechanics of the pitching delivery. In pitching vernacular, "mechanics" means the proper, balanced synchronization of our body parts (arms, legs, feet, head) and movements prior to and after the delivery of the pitch. Establishing good balance and good body position is an essential ingredient of good pitching. It allows us to be less reliant on timing, a quality not constant enough to be reliable.

Also, pay close attention to what I've written about how to properly throw the most common pitches—fastball, change-up, and curveball. Solid pitching mechanics are great, but if a player's pitches are sub-par, he'll have trouble getting batters out. During practice you should strike an appropriate balance between mechanics and pitch development.

Most, if not all, of the chapters should be read, contemplated, and read again. Please don't expect to immediately grasp every concept. Twenty-game winners aren't built in a day. Your pitchers need to practice their delivery and their pitches over and over again. Correct, repetitive practice is the key to improving.

The mere fact that you purchased this book tells me you'd like to better understand the art and science of pitching. You're interested in gaining knowledge that you can pass on to the players. That's a big part of being a coach. The kids will be forever grateful.

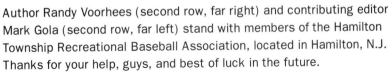

Author Randy Voorhees (second row, far right) and contributing editor Mark Gola (second row, far left) stand with members of the Hamilton Township Recreational Baseball Association, located in Hamilton, N.J. Thanks for your help, guys, and best of luck in the future.

GOOD PITCHING BEATS GOOD HITTING

"Good pitching beats good hitting" is among the truest, most time-tested sports axioms ever uttered. Pitchers are critical to deciding the outcome of a baseball game—so critical that one will be recorded as the winner and one as the loser. No other player in any team sport is officially designated the winner or loser of a game.

At no level of baseball is the pitcher more important than in Little League. A good Little League pitcher—one who consistently throws strikes with something on the ball—will dominate the game. Conversely, some Little League games deteriorate into "walkathons" because the pitchers cannot throw strikes. The difference between good and poor pitching at this age level is most often a factor of how much proper training a pitcher has received.

If good pitching is so critical to the team's success, and therefore to players' greater enjoyment of the game, it makes sense to devote plenty of time to properly training pitchers. As coaches we must devote ourselves to identifying the most logical pitching candidates (often the biggest players or those with the strongest arms). Then, we must help those players develop their arms, their pitching mechanics, and their pitches.

Consistently throwing strikes keeps the game moving and the defense on their toes.

Identifying, training, and developing pitchers will benefit more than just the kids on the mound. Every player will benefit directly from a good performance by the pitcher. Consider these facts:

- When the pitcher is consistently throwing good strikes, the fielders are always alert and ready to make a play. They have to be, because the ball might be put into play on any pitch. The shortstop can't afford to be back on his heels and the right fielder doesn't have time to search for the best cloverleaf to pick up. When the pitcher is always around the plate, the fielders make plays they wouldn't otherwise make. This builds their confidence and enhances their enjoyment of the game.
- Good pitching certainly makes life easier on the catcher. He makes fewer trips to the backstop to retrieve errant pitches, and, most important, he doesn't have to make that tiring and

debilitating squat as many times. A rested, alert catcher makes the game crisper and cleaner.

- Every player loves to bat. When the pitcher performs well, it means that his teammates get back to the dugout sooner. There is less time between at-bats.

- A good pitcher shortens the game. No more three-hour marathons that stretch the endurance of children, who aren't famous for their patience or attention span. Short, crisp games make the parents and coaches happy, too!

> Nobody likes to hear it, because it's dull. But the reason you win or lose is darn near always the same . . . pitching.
>
> —Earl Weaver, former major league manager

Identifying Pitchers

Once you've established the goal of training and developing good pitchers, you must identify a number of prospects. The most obvious candidates are those players who have prior pitching experience. Beyond that, here are some other factors to consider during your search:

- *Throwing form and accuracy.* Observe your players as they warm up or perform in drills. Invariably, some players will throw with better form and accuracy, two of the essential ingredients for a good pitcher. There's a big difference between a thrower and a pitcher. Learn to distinguish between the two.

- *Arm strength.* Again, watch the players as they warm up. Make a note of which kids have the strongest arms. A strong arm is an obvious asset for a pitcher. A player with an unusually strong arm, even with form and accuracy problems, may be developed into a pitcher.
- *Size.* Young pitchers come in all shapes and sizes. Although size should never be an insurmountable obstacle for a would-be pitcher, height and strength are undeniably assets for a pitcher. Give me a choice between a good big pitcher and a good small pitcher, and I'll take the big guy every time.
- *Competitiveness.* Look for the players who have a competitive spirit. Put them through some games (races, throwing competitions, scrimmages) and see who really wants to win. Since the pitching position is the most important in baseball, it comes with a lot of responsibility and, yes, pressure. Remember that in baseball not only does the team get a "W" or "L," the pitcher gets one too. That can be a lot for a kid to handle. Only competitive people need apply.
- *Overall attitude.* Show me someone who is open to learning, adaptable, smart, and eager; someone who is interested in improving; accepts responsibility; and has at least a modicum of athletic ability; and I'll show you someone who can be a pitcher. Most pitchers are made, not born, but to become a good pitcher you have to want to be a good pitcher.

A Commitment to Pitching

If you agree with the premise that pitching is the most important prerequisite for team success, then it should receive your greatest attention. You will improve in direct proportion to the level at which you emphasize pitching. Set aside time for developing pitchers in every practice you schedule. Develop a mantra: "Our team will go as far as our pitchers take us."

There are no shortcuts to building arm strength. You must throw regularly.

AN ADVANCED GAME OF CATCH

One easy way to assess the pitching potential of players is to ask them to play a special, advanced game of catch. In this game of catch there are two rules that don't normally apply: (1) Each player must go through the pitching delivery (from the set position, not the full windup) every time he throws the ball. (2) The players must always throw the ball at the area in front of their partner's chest or face. Players get one point for each time they "hit" the chest target and two points for each time they hit the face target. The first player to 31 points wins. This game will allow you to observe the form, arm strength, accuracy, and competitiveness of the players.

A Foundation for Great Pitching

To build anything you must first lay a foundation, and every foundation requires solid cornerstones. I believe there are four cornerstones to great pitching. They are listed below in order of importance.

1. *Command.* The ability to precisely locate your pitches.
2. *Changing speeds.* As the great Hall of Fame pitcher Warren Spahn said, "Hitting is timing. Pitching is upsetting timing." It pays to keep the batters off balance.
3. *Movement.* It's much easier for the batter to make solid contact with a straight pitch. Learn how to make the ball tail, sink, or cut.
4. *Velocity.* Pitches traveling at a higher rate of speed afford the batter less time to determine whether or not to swing and less time to execute a swing. (Notice, however, that velocity is ranked only fourth. Velocity in and of itself is not enough to guarantee a consistently good performance.)

7

Just take the ball and throw it where you want to. Throw strikes. Home plate don't move.

—Satchel Paige, Hall of Fame pitcher

If you command your pitches, you will be successful. If you command your pitches and change speeds, you will be more successful. If you command your pitches, change speeds, and generate movement on your pitches—particularly your fastball—you will be a consistent winner. If you master all four cornerstones of pitching, you will be a hitter's nightmare.

A radar gun is useful for measuring the improvement of a pitcher's velocity.

The Pitcher's Routine

Now that you've made the commitment to pitching excellence, you must create a daily routine. Pitchers should throw the ball every day. Put together a schedule of soft tossing (playing catch), long tossing, throwing from the bullpen mound, form throwing, and drills for pitching mechanics. Here's a sample in-season throwing program for a Little League pitcher:

8

Monday	Pitch six innings in a game
Tuesday	Play catch (40–50 feet) for 10 to 15 minutes
Wednesday	Long toss (30–60–90 feet) for 10 to 15 minutes
Thursday	Go to the bullpen mound and practice mechanics and pitches for 15 minutes
Friday	Play catch for 10 to 15 minutes
Saturday	Long toss for 10 to 15 minutes
Sunday	Off
Monday	Pitch six innings in a game

Special Treatment

It is undeniable that pitchers hold a special place on the team. Shouldn't they, then, receive some special treatment? Here are some ways to emphasize their special status:

- Schedule practices for pitchers and catchers only.
- Designate yourself or one of your coaching colleagues as the team's "pitching coach."

LEVEL-THREE STRIKES

Andy Lopez, a very successful baseball coach at Pepperdine University and the University of Florida, has developed a system for grading the strikes his pitchers throw. A level-one strike is a pitch located over the center of the plate. A level-two strike is one located above the knees and over one of the corners of the plate. A level-three strike is one located at the knees and over one of the corners of the plate. Lopez wants all his pitchers to throw as many level-three strikes as possible. That should be the goal for your pitchers, too.

- Buy and use a pitching chart to quantify and qualify the strikes they throw in practices and games. Everyone loves to see tangible evidence of improvement.
- Bring a camcorder to practice and record pitching deliveries both before and after focused training. The differences are often striking. Buy and use pitching books and videotapes, too.
- If you have access to a radar gun, use it. Pick your spots, though. Bring it out when you believe it will show an improvement in velocity. That will surely bring a smile to a kid's face, and some renewed motivation, too.
- Praise your pitchers constantly. I can't say it enough: praise, praise, praise, even while you're correcting. It doesn't take much to make a pitcher feel special; once he does, he'll do almost anything you ask.

Now that you've identified the pitching prospects and devised a plan for training and developing them, it's time to get down to specifics. We'll start with the mechanics of the pitching delivery.

Videotape provides an excellent way for a coach to review a pitcher's performance. It also allows the pitcher to see himself in action. This also greatly helps communication between teacher and student.

> They're [pitchers] the only ones on the diamond who have high ground. That's symbolic. You know what they tell you in a war: "Take the high ground first."
>
> —Richie Ashburn, Hall of Fame player

2

THE MECHANICS OF THE PITCHING DELIVERY

"Mechanics" are the moving parts of a pitcher's delivery. This term can be confusing and intimidating for a young pitcher, so I've created a definition that's simple: Mechanics are how a pitcher moves his body from the beginning of his delivery to the end. Good mechanics mean that these movements are balanced, synchronized, and performed in proper sequence. This doesn't guarantee high-quality pitches, but it sure helps. Rarely can a pitcher consistently deliver good pitches without solid mechanics. Mechanics are the pitcher's foundation upon which we add other building blocks such as arm strength (velocity and endurance), location, movement, diversity of pitches, and mental acuity and toughness.

Keep It Simple

Before you begin your pitching delivery, you must first get a good grip on the baseball. (All of the most popular grips are described in detail in subsequent chapters.) Grip the ball with your fingers, not your palm. Your grip should be firm but not tight, and your

wrist should remain loose and flexible. Now you're ready to pitch the ball.

The pitching delivery is really a chain reaction of events, each movement intertwined with the one before and after. One failure in the chain may lead to a breakdown. By making your movements as simple to perform and as few as possible, you decrease the chances of a flaw. Thus, I recommend that Little League pitchers pitch exclusively from the set position, also known as the stretch position. Do away with the windup; it provides no tangible benefits. If you don't believe me, check with Mariano Rivera, the New York Yankee reliever who is widely considered the best in the game. He pitches exclusively from the set position, even though he often enters the game with no runners on base. If the windup delivery were superior in any way to the set-position delivery, a superb professional such as Rivera would use it.

The Set Position

The set position doesn't require a rocker step or a pivot, the two movements that often cause pitchers to get into unbalanced positions. Because it's much easier to maintain your balance working from the set position, you can throw more strikes. Also, contrary to popular belief, pitchers can throw just as hard from the set position as they do from the windup. Thus, pitchers gain accuracy without losing any velocity.

The set position is easy to establish. Simply place the outside of your pivot foot against the pitching rubber and your stride foot shoulder-width distance away in the direction of the plate. Hold the ball in your glove directly in front of your chest. All points on the glove side of your body are closed to the target. You should look directly over your lead shoulder at the target. Your weight should be evenly distributed between your two feet. You are now prepared to begin your delivery.

I believe that fewer Little League pitchers should use the full windup.

Notice how the pitcher's weight remains balanced over the rubber as he takes his rocker step. Young pitchers often make the mistake of shifting their weight back, which can produce problems with balance later in the delivery.

The Four Stages of the Delivery

I have divided the delivery into four stages:

1. Knee raise and foot press
2. Ball separation and glide step
3. Landing, forward armswing, glove-arm pull
4. Extension and finish

The first two stages are preparatory, getting your body into the best position to throw a baseball powerfully and accurately. The third stage includes the actual delivery of the pitch. Stage four is

A LITTLE SOMETHING TO GET YOU STARTED

For most people it's difficult to perform an athletic movement from a dead still position. For example, golfers often perform a "waggle" of the club before beginning their swing. A waggle is a gentle back and forth movement of the shaft and club-head (and often the golfer's feet and hips, too) that removes tension from the body. Pitchers, too, should consider making a tension-relieving move prior to starting their delivery.

One way is to begin with your feet wider than shoulder-width and your hands at your sides. Next, bring your hands together at your chest while moving your stride foot back to a position shoulder-width from your pivot foot. This little "pitcher's waggle" is a way to ensure that the first move of your delivery—the knee raise—is performed without any tension in the body.

when you finish your delivery with a sound follow-through. Each stage is crucial. A breakdown anywhere may compromise the entire delivery. No stage should be treated as more or less important than any other.

Stage One

The knee raise. The delivery from the set position begins with a simple raise of the stride-leg knee. Raise your knee until your upper leg is belt-high, your foot is hanging directly below your knee (with your foot flat or your toes pointed down), and your stride-leg hip is rotated slightly, so that your catcher can see your back pocket, but not the number on the back of your jersey. Your post-leg knee is flexed slightly, but you must stay tall with your upper body. Your hands are directly in front of your chest with your head on the tar-

Raise your knee just above your waistline while keeping your upper body tall. The post leg (the left leg for a left-handed pitcher) is slightly flexed to maintain balance.

get. You must be able to stop at this position during the delivery, perfectly balanced with all your weight on your pivot foot.

The foot press. Once you have completed the knee raise, the next step in the delivery is the foot press. Simply press your stride foot back down toward the ground, to a position just a few inches from the surface of the mound. This is the step that many young pitchers forget. Instead, they begin to stride toward the plate before pressing down. What they are doing is engaging in the most common and destructive pitching flaw of all: rushing.

Rushing is the premature movement of the upper-body toward the plate, the result of which is a lower, weaker arm position and a loss of power and control. Here is an easy way to remember the proper sequence of body movements: what goes up (knee raise) must come down (foot press). You should also be able to stop at the foot-press position of the delivery, perfectly balanced with all your weight still on your pivot foot. You are now ready to begin stage two of the pitching delivery.

Stage Two

Ball separation. The instant you complete the foot press and begin gliding toward the target, you remove the ball from your glove and swing it down, back, and up into throwing position (commonly referred to as the "high-cocked" or "power" position). Your arm finishes in a position with your throwing elbow at shoulder-height with your hand "showing" the ball to the center fielder. Your elbow is flexed and your arm is as free from tension as possible.

After you remove the ball from your glove, extend your glove arm down the target line, until it's nearly shoulder-height. Show the batter the back of your wrist, so that the glove does not obscure your vision of the target. With the ball at the high-cocked position and your glove arm extended down the target line, you are now in the power position.

The pitcher poses in the "high-cocked" or "power" position. The throwing elbow is at shoulder-height, and the hand is showing the ball to the center fielder.

The glide step. Only after you have pressed your stride foot down do you begin to glide toward the plate. Notice that I use the word "glide." *There is no pushing off the rubber involved, no lunging toward the plate.* Rather, you effortlessly glide down the slope of the mound toward your target. The glide step is little more than a controlled fall, with gravity helping you to keep your body quiet and tension free. All points on the front side of your body (shoulder, hip, knee, foot) remain closed to the target during the glide step.

It is crucial that you initiate the glide step with the lower half of your body, specifically the outside of your stride foot. Keep the upper half of your body back. Stay tall with your upper body. This is what people mean when you hear them tell you to "stay back." This helps you avoid rushing.

The length of your glide step is largely a product of your height. The taller you are, the longer your glide step should be. For young

After lowering your leg from the knee-raise position, the stride leg glides out toward the target. The glide step is little more than a controlled fall.

pitchers, the minimum length of the glide step should be roughly 80–90 percent of body height. That is, the stride length for a pitcher five feet tall should be 48–54 inches. A glide step that is too short produces pitches in the dirt, and overstriding usually produces pitches high and out of the strike zone.

Stage Three

The landing. The glide step concludes when your stride foot touches the ground. How you land your foot on the ground is important. You should land flat-footed or on the balls of your feet, but never on your heel. A heel landing is jarring to the body and adversely affects balance.

For a right-handed pitcher, your foot should land either directly on the target line or slightly to the right. You must never land to the glove side of the target line. That is called an open landing, a very weak and unbalanced position to throw from. Your toe should point to the 1:00 position (for a right-hander; 11:00 for a left-hander). All points on the front side of your body—shoulder, hip, knee, and toe—should be closed to the target at landing, just as they were during the entire glide-step phase.

Forward armswing. As your stride foot hits the ground, your throwing arm and hand move forward toward the target. How fast should your arm and hand move? As fast as you can move them and still maintain body balance and control of your pitches. Your throwing elbow remains at least as high as shoulder-height until no

In the power position, the baseball faces center field.

earlier than release of the pitch. At release, your fingers are behind and over the baseball. You throw the ball on a down angle to the batter, with no conscious slowing of your arm. (Your arm has "decelerator muscles," which provide for a natural slowing of the arm after the ball is gone.) The spot at which the ball leaves your hand, known as the "release point," should be the same on every pitch.

Glove-arm pull. At the same time that you move your throwing arm forward, pull your glove arm directly back toward your body. You simply turn the fingers of your glove toward the sky and pull your elbow down and into your side. At release, your glove-side shoulder is lower than your throwing shoulder, but both are perpendicular to the target line. This pulling action complements the pushing action created by throwing the ball. Now your upper body is powerfully rotating, one side pushing and the other side pulling.

THE RADAR GUN

Many radar guns work by measuring the velocity of the pitch the instant it leaves the pitcher's hand. Students of physics know that this means that the radar gun is actually measuring the speed of the pitcher's hand at release point. This means that when Roger Clemens throws a 95-mile-per-hour fastball, his hand is traveling at 95 miles per hour when he releases the ball. (Hand speed equals pitch speed.) Thus, assuming that the mechanics of your delivery are sound, once your stride foot hits the ground there is only one determining factor for the velocity of the pitch: how fast you can move your throwing arm and hand. Nothing else will provide you with additional power—not a big rotation, a leg kick, or a push off the rubber. Maximize your arm and hand speed, and watch your velocity increase.

In addition to adding power to the delivery, the glove-arm pull balances your body. Minus any action with your glove arm, the violent action of your forward armswing creates an imbalance in your body—one side working hard and one side dormant.

Stage Four

Extension. After you release the pitch, extend your throwing arm down and across the target line (and your body) until you finish with your hand across the mid-to-lower part of your stride leg. Extending your arm as far in front of your body as possible will help to ensure that there is no unnatural deceleration of your arm. This extension also helps not only to fire your post leg toward the target but also to snap your upper body over and into the pitch.

The forceful momentum of your armswing will pull your entire body into the pitch. There should be no recoiling of the arm or any other intentional slowing of this good momentum.

Finish. The finish position varies from pitcher to pitcher, according to variables such as individual physiology, the position of the arm and hand at release, and arm and hand speed at release. Generally speaking, though, your pivot foot should finish past the stride foot and on or close to the target line. Your upper body should be bent at least slightly forward, with your throwing arm across the target line and your throwing hand at least approaching the stride-leg knee. Your head should be up, with your eyes still locked on the target. You've gone from "tall to small."

Pulling with your glove arm is essential to generating maximum arm speed and velocity on your pitches.

Whatever your finish looks like, it must be natural. Too many pitchers contrive their finishes to satisfy the demands of parents and coaches who admonish, "Bend your back." The forward momentum of your armswing will snap your upper body over, thus bending your back. Don't worry about bending your back; it will bend on its own if the rest of your delivery is sound. If you throw the pitch correctly, the finish will usually take care of itself.

The Winds of Change

Over the past few decades, many of the long-held imperatives of good pitching mechanics have been abandoned in favor of new body movements and positions. Not that many years ago, pitching experts believed that pushing off the rubber, collapsing the post leg, and the 12:00–6:00 arm slot were all essential elements of good pitching. Now, largely because of videotape and the study of biomechanics, these elements are no longer taught. Coaches and parents must follow these winds of change, so that they are providing players with only the most current, correct information. The following are parts of the pitching doctrine that have gone the way of the dinosaur and the sandlot baseball game.

This is an excellent example of proper positioning at the point of release.

Collapsing the Post (Back) Leg

Collapsing the back leg is the "drop" part of the "drop and drive" delivery made famous by Hall of Fame pitcher Tom Seaver. Collapsing on your back leg makes it difficult to maintain your balance and difficult to throw a good breaking ball, and, perhaps most important, reduces your body height. This means that your pitches travel on a flat trajectory. Instead, you should maintain your body height—stay tall—so that your pitches travel on a downward plane toward the batter.

Pushing Off the Rubber

Pushing off the rubber is the "drive" part of the drop and drive delivery. Pushing off the rubber only leads to rushing, the most

Extending your throwing arm down and across the target line is crucial to producing consistent strikes thrown at maximum velocity. The throwing arm finishes across the mid-to-lower part of your stride leg.

Once you finish your pitch, you become the eighth fielder out on the diamond.

23

common and disastrous of pitching flaws, where your upper body is prematurely driven toward the target. The results are a dragging or slinging arm action, overstriding, and recoiling of the arm after delivery. This movement is neither powerful nor balanced. It's much better to execute a controlled fall toward the target.

Throwing Overhand

Years ago coaches instructed their players to "throw overhand," or "over the top." They wanted the highest arm slot possible, the "12:00–6:00" position. Coaches believed that throwing from a lower position, particularly sidearm, would be harmful to pitchers' arms. Nothing could be further from the truth.

Here is an example of a pitcher collapsing his back leg. The throwing elbow often drops below the shoulder, causing the pitcher to get "underneath" his pitches. This produces pitches up in, or up and out of, the strike zone.

When the pitcher attempts to push off the rubber, his body rushes out to home plate, never allowing his throwing arm to catch up and stay on top of the ball.

This is the correct way to stay in balance and execute a controlled fall toward the target.

The human arm is not designed to throw overhand. It is designed to throw underhand, the way a softball pitcher throws. (This is why it is not uncommon for softball pitchers to pitch both ends of a doubleheader.) The higher you raise your arm, the more stressful throwing becomes on your shoulder. Also, the higher arm slot position makes it more difficult to create movement on your pitches. Batters run for the bat rack when they see a pitcher coming "straight over the top." Find something in the three-quarter-arm slot position and stick with it.

Reaching Back

Reaching back is extending your throwing arm down and back in an attempt to generate more power. It was believed that creating a greater distance for the ball to travel before reaching the release point would allow more time for your throwing arm to accelerate,

Reaching back to gain more power is counterproductive and places the pitcher in an awkward position.

meaning more velocity on the pitch. In reality, reaching back puts the pitcher in a very awkward position, with his shoulders tilted instead of level and his arm dragging behind. In fact, it takes very little distance or time for the throwing arm and hand to reach maximum velocity. A shorter down, back, and up movement is much more efficient.

Turn Your Back on the Batter

"Turn your back on the batter" is another way of saying that you should coil your body as you raise your leg at the beginning of the delivery. Coaches once believed that this early coiling would deliver more power to the delivery. Slight turning is good, but too much is disastrous. As you reach the top of your leg raise, the catcher should be able to see your left back pocket (for a right-handed pitcher), but not the number on the back of your jersey.

27

Striding closed blocks the pitcher's hips and forces him to throw across his body.

Striding open rotates the hips prematurely and puts unnecessary strain on the pitcher's throwing elbow.

Striding down the target line is the optimum position for accuracy and maximum velocity; it also minimizes stress on the pitching arm.

Too much rotation means that you'll have to swing your stride leg instead of pressing it straight down and gliding directly toward the target. Swinging often results in your stride foot landing too far to the left or right of the target line, and that's very bad. Too much rotation also means that your shoulders will be tilted away from the target line, and you'll need perfect timing to ensure that they are on or parallel to the target line at landing. Timing, remember, is too ephemeral to be relied upon.

Overstriding

Coaches used to fret frequently about a pitcher's stride being too long. Now, through the use of video analysis, we've discovered that a longer stride is usually best. Power pitchers, in fact, often stride distances greater than their body height. As long as you keep your upper body tall and your body in good balance, you should be able to stride as far as you want and still deliver strikes. Also, the closer you land to the plate, the less distance your pitches have to travel and the less time the batter has to execute his swing. Overstriding was a product of pushing off the rubber, and since we don't do that anymore, we don't see many overstriding pitchers.

Finish in Perfect Fielding Position

I still hear coaches instructing their pitchers to finish their deliveries in perfect fielding position. This "square landing" is too conservative for me. It is a contrived finish position in which the pitcher is asked to decelerate his body. The momentum established by the pitcher's armswing and glove pull should result in a more aggressive finish, with the pitcher's post leg and pivot foot finishing past his stride foot and on or across the target line. This is a much more natural finish. The pitcher is still able to defend his position. (Note: The more powerful the pitcher, the less able he is to finish in a square landing. Some finesse pitchers who rely less on power may be able to naturally land square.)

Pitching Drills

There are dozens of drills that you can and should use to improve your delivery. Most require little more than soft throwing, and none require you to throw with maximum exertion. Pick out your favorites and do them every time you go to the field. It shouldn't take you more than a few minutes, and it's time well spent.

One-Knee Drill (simple)

Place the knee of your post leg (right knee for a right-handed pitcher) on the ground with your stride foot flat on the ground for balance. Hold your glove directly in front of your chest with your hand holding the ball in the glove. Rotate your shoulders and separate into the power position. Now deliver the pitch, making sure to extend your throwing arm down and across your stride leg and to pull your glove arm down and into your side.

One-Knee Drill (advanced)

Everything is the same as above, except that as you deliver the pitch, you must transfer the weight of your upper body out over your stride leg so that you can stand up as you finish your armswing.

Balance Drill

Take a soft rocker step, pivot in front of the rubber, lift the stride leg, and hold for ten seconds. Repeat ten times.

The one-knee pitching drill

Balance and Glide Drill

Balance on your post leg with the stride leg in the perfect lift position (foot hanging directly under the knee). Press your stride foot down and back twice without touching the ground, then press it down a third time, glide down the target line, and deliver the pitch.

Throw and Finish Drill

Set up in the power position with your feet slightly more than shoulder-width apart. You're simulating the position in which you land during the delivery. Throw the ball without moving your stride foot forward, making sure to get maximum arm extension and good glove-side pull, and pivoting on your stride foot. Check your finish position to make sure it's what you want.

Wall Drill

Stand with your back to a wall (or fence), about six inches away. Separate your hands into the power position. Your throwing arm

The balance and glide drill

or hand should not touch the wall. If you make contact with the wall, your throwing arm is not making the correct down, back, and up swing. Swinging too far behind your body may be caused by several things, including separating your hands too far from your body or over-rotating at the top of your leg raise. It may also be the result of poor initial alignment. Make sure that you don't line up too close to the target.

The throw and finish drill

The wall (or fence) drill

Mechanics Evaluation Form

You should develop a mechanics evaluation form for every pitcher on the team. Observe the pitcher over several practice sessions and complete a written assessment of his delivery, then share the information with the pitcher. Putting something in writing gives it more weight. It also provides a benchmark for calculating the pitcher's progress; it's the beginning of "before and after." Include the following items on your form:

- Pitcher's name, age, and whether he throws left-handed or right-handed
- Grips for all pitches
- Leg raise
- Foot press
- Separation (ball from glove)
- Glide step
- Glove action
- Hand and arm slot
- Landing position
- Forward arm extension
- Trunk rotation
- Finish position
- Velocity for all pitches

This sequence illustrates two important elements to the pitcher's motion: balance and simplicity. Notice how the pitcher raises his knee and lowers it straight back down before executing a controlled glide out toward home plate. The pitcher correctly releases the ball out in front of his body (next page) and achieves full extension after releasing the pitch.

35

3

THE FASTBALL

The fastball is the most important pitch in baseball. If you can command your fastball, that is, put it where you want it when you want it, you will be successful—guaranteed. In fact, if you have consistent command of your fastball, you can be successful even when your other pitches aren't working. Conversely, if you can't consistently command your fastball, you haven't yet earned the right to be called a pitcher.

The evidence in support of the fastball being the most important pitch is strong and plentiful. Consider these facts:

- The fastball is the easiest pitch to learn. Gripping a fastball is simple and the release requires only a loose, straight wrist position. It is the "pitch" that we throw the first time we pick up and toss a ball.
- The fastball is the easiest pitch to throw for a strike. The fastball travels on the straightest line, at the highest velocity, and is the most common pitch; therefore it's easiest to control.
- The fastball travels at the highest velocity of any pitch, which means the batter has the least amount of time to see the ball.
- The fastball is the pitch that all batters prefer to swing at, so it generates more swings, and that means more opportunities for outs.

- Unlike any other pitch, the fastball can be made to move in three directions—down, in, or out. Sinking fastballs, tailing fastballs, and cutting fastballs all present different challenges for the batter.
- The fastball is the only pitch that is successfully thrown in all four major pitch locations—down, up, in, and out. (You wouldn't intentionally throw an off-speed pitch high in the strike zone, would you?)
- The fastball sets up your off-speed pitches. The change-up and curveball are companion pitches to the fastball, designed to make the batter believe the pitch is a fastball. If you have command of your fastball, your off-speed pitches will be tough to resist.
- Thrown properly, with sound mechanics, the fastball is the only pitch that helps build arm strength.
- You can win a game with only your fastball. If you can throw the pitch with good location, good movement, and sufficient velocity, you don't need another pitch. Of course, if you can do all those things with your fastball *and* throw another pitch for strikes, you'll win almost any game.

39

About the only thing wrong with the fastball is its name. The word "fastball" gives the impression that velocity is the most important quality of the pitch. It isn't. It is much more important that you locate the fastball where you want it. Second most important is that you throw the pitch with movement—in, out, or down. Velocity is the least important quality of the fastball, so maybe we should rename the pitch. How does "real estate pitch" sound? (The most important thing in real estate is location, location, location, and if you're looking at real estate, you're planning to move.) That may sound silly, but no less an authority than Greg Maddux, a four-time Cy Young Award winner, has described himself as a "real estate pitcher."

Get a Grip on It

The velocity and movement of your fastball is largely a product of how well you grip the ball. Gripping the ball correctly—firmly in your fingers (not your palm) with a loose wrist and forearm—enables you to impart maximum rotation on the ball. Good rotation means good speed and good movement.

There are many varieties of fastball. You should perfect at least two of them. Experiment to find out which fastballs are best for you.

The Four-Seam Fastball

There are at least five fastball grips, each of which is employed with a specific purpose—mostly to generate movement. The one exception is the four-seam grip, the most common, which is used to throw a comparatively straight fastball. The four-seam fastball is not only the straightest pitch, it's the fastest; hence, it's the easiest to throw for a strike, and it arrives at the plate in the least amount of time. Every young pitcher should master the four-seam fastball before any other pitch.

40

The pitcher is poised to deliver a four-seam fastball.

How to grip it. Grip the four-seam fastball by placing the pads of your index and middle fingers across the seam of the ball, far enough over the seam so that you can gain leverage by pulling back on the seam to generate backspin. (Backspin is what gives the pitch carry and velocity.) Spread these two fingers approximately an inch apart. Experiment with the positioning of these fingers so that you get maximum rotation and maximum velocity.

Grip the ball firmly but without tension. Your thumb rests on the underside of the ball, at a position between your index and middle fingers. Your ring finger rests against the side of the ball and should not be engaged at all in throwing the pitch. Your pinky finger should not touch the ball. (Note: If you have very small hands, you may need to use three fingers to throw this pitch. Place them so that your middle finger is on an imaginary line running

Grip the four-seam fastball by placing the pads of your index and middle fingers across the ball. Your ring finger rests on the side of the ball, and your thumb is positioned on the underside of the ball.

through the middle of the ball.) Check to make sure that there is minimal contact between the ball and your palm. Palm contact causes friction, thereby reducing velocity. It also reduces "feel." You get much better feel for the ball with your fingers than with your palm. At release, think about pulling down on the seams as you throw the back and top of the ball.

When and how to use it. Because the four-seam fastball is your straightest pitch, it is also the easiest pitch for batters to hit, so you must understand how to use it best. Throw it when you must have a strike, for example, or to hitters who simply can't handle the velocity. It's also useful for trying to jam hitters, because a straight fastball thrown inside will stay there; it won't move out over the plate where it can be hit hard.

The Two-Seam Fastball

The second most common fastball grip is the two-seam grip. This pitch generally provides tailing action (moves in toward a same-hand hitter), and sometimes it sinks, too. It's called a two-seam fastball because your index and middle fingers are each positioned on top of the seam. The pitch is best thrown from a three-quarter-arm slot. If your arm slot positions your hand any closer to your head at release, you won't generate the movement you're looking for.

How to grip it. Grip the ball along the seams where they are closest together, placing your thumb underneath on an imaginary line running through the center of the ball. Place a little more pressure on the ball with your index finger, and at release think about throwing the inside of the ball. This will promote a tailing action on the ball.

When and how to use it. The two-seam fastball doesn't rotate as quickly as the four-seam fastball, so it doesn't travel as fast. But what it lacks in velocity, it makes up for in movement. Your target should be low in the strike zone. This is the perfect pitch for when

Grip the two-seam fastball along the seams where they are closest together. The two-seam fastball travels at a lesser velocity, but generates movement.

you are trying to cause a ground ball. Because of the downward movement of the pitch, you may also generate a swing and miss (over the ball).

The Sinking Fastball (Sinker)

Another effective fastball is the sinking fastball, or sinker. This pitch dives down—"sinks"—as it enters the strike zone. The sinker is thrown with a variation of the two-seam grip.

How to grip it. Instead of placing your index and middle fingers on top of the seams where they are closest, place those fingers across the seams where they are closest. Again, the idea is to exert more pressure on the ball with your index finger and try to visualize throwing the inside of the ball. The natural pronation of your wrist at release will help the ball get the rotation you want.

43

To throw a sinking fastball, grip the ball across the seams where they are closest. Place more pressure on your index finger and visualize throwing the inside of the ball.

When and how to use it. The sinker does not require great velocity to be an effective pitch. In fact, you may get more movement on the pitch by throwing it at less than full speed. Remember, you're throwing this pitch in an attempt to generate contact—preferably a ground ball—and not a swing and miss.

The Cut Fastball (Cutter)

The cut fastball, or cutter, is the only fastball that breaks away from a same-hand hitter. A cut fastball can be a tremendously effective pitch, because the hitter sees one fastball that bores in on him, another that runs away from him, and another that is straight. It is also a good pitch for jamming an opposite-hand hitter, because the ball has late movement in toward his hands.

How to grip it. The most common way to grip the cutter is to modify your four-seam grip by moving all of your fingers, including your thumb, to the right (for a right-handed pitcher). Bring your

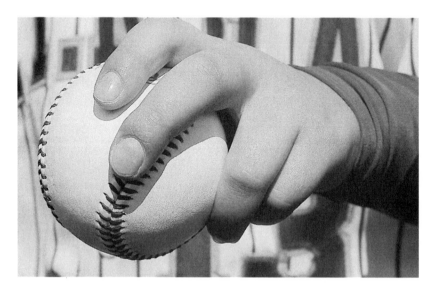

To throw a cut fastball, simply modify your four-seam fastball grip. Move all of your fingers, including your thumb, to the left (for a left-handed pitcher).

index and middle fingers together. Because you are gripping the ball off-center, you should see much of the ball sticking out of the inside of your hand. At release, you want to throw the high and outside part of the ball with a fastball arm-swing.

When and how to use it. Experiment with the pitch until you get the movement you want. The cutter will break horizontally more than vertically. A well-thrown cutter won't break that much, but the break will be quick and late, ideally after the batter has already begun his swing. You can run this pitch away from a same-hand hitter or into an opposite-hand hitter. When properly located— away from the center of the plate—you'll avoid the sweet spot of the bat. You'll see balls weakly hit off the handle or end of the bat.

FORGET THE SPLITTER

The best thing I can say to a young pitcher about gripping a splitter is—don't. Generally, young pitchers don't have hands big enough to grip the pitch properly, and much evidence suggests that this pitch may be bad for your arm. Leave the splitter to older players, the ones who get paid to pitch.

The Mechanics of the Fastball

Like any other pitch, the key to throwing your best fastball is solid mechanics. That is, you must synchronize your body movements and maintain good balance so that you are in the best position to throw the ball accurately and forcefully. (Please refer back to Chapter 2 for a more detailed, thorough description of the pitching delivery.) Let's review the stages of the pitching delivery that will have the most impact on the quality of your fastball.

The Leg Raise

Your leg raise should be as compact and simple as possible. Lift your stride leg so that your upper leg is parallel with the ground, your knee points at third base (for a right-handed pitcher), and your foot is directly under your knee with your toes pointing anywhere but up. Be careful not to over-rotate during your lift phase. (For a right-handed pitcher the catcher should be able to see your left back pocket, but not the numbers of the back of your jersey.) Over-rotating causes you to swing your leg as you begin your stride, and that often results in landing in a very closed position—too far to the right for a right-handed pitcher. From that position you will be forced to throw across your body. Throwing across your body places too much stress on your arm, and you can't generate maximum power or accuracy.

Separation and Backswing

Remove the ball from your glove—separate your hands—as you lower your stride leg (from the top of the leg raise); separate at a point between your belly button and chest. Quickly swing the ball down, back, and up in a small arc, until you reach the high-cocked position. This movement should be relatively short. At this point, your throwing elbow should be at shoulder height, and your throwing hand should be "showing" the ball to second base. Your fingers are behind and on top of the ball. Do not swing your arm behind your body. The ball comes out of your glove in front of your body and moves backward on a straight line. From this powerful position you are prepared to begin your glide to the plate.

Glide

Your stride foot leads you toward the plate by gliding low to the ground on a line either directly to the plate or slightly to the right

As you lower your leg from the knee lift, separate your throwing hand from your glove to start your armswing.

(for a right-handed pitcher) of a straight line. Try to have your upper body trail your lower body. You should feel your weight remain on your back foot for as long as possible. This is called "staying back." This is crucial, because if your upper body moves forward too early or too forcefully, your throwing arm will never catch up. The result will most often be a bad pitch, usually high and in to your arm side.

Pulling

As your stride foot lands and you begin to rotate your upper body in preparation for releasing the pitch, you must remember to pull your glove-side elbow back into your side. This pulling action balances the upper-body rotation, making it more powerful. Failing to pull with your elbow makes you a one-sided pitcher. That is, only one side of your body—your arm side—is participating in the powerful upper-body rotation that happens just prior to releasing the pitch. One-sided pitchers sacrifice balance and power.

Release

Try to hit the same arm slot and release point for every pitch. I prefer the three-quarter-arm slot. Keep your hand away from your head. It is very difficult to generate movement from a release point close to your head, and this "12:00–6:00" position is very stressful on the throwing shoulder. Your fingers, wrist, and forearm should be as relaxed as possible at release. You accomplish this by not trying to throw too hard. "Reaching back" for more power will do little more than bring tension, which slows the pitch down. Use the seams at release—pull on them to generate as much rotation on the ball as possible. Remember, more rotation means more velocity and more movement.

Extension

After releasing the pitch, your throwing arm extends down and across your body, finishing in a position across or below your stride-leg knee. This is the opposite of the short armswing you make as you separate the ball from your glove. Here is the rule: short in back, long in front. Think about throwing the ball *through* the catcher, not to him.

The eyes (and head) stay focused on the target after release.

Pivot and Fire the Backside

Your stride foot lands in a slightly closed position at the end of the glide phase. Now, as you release the pitch, pivot on your stride foot, turning it left (for a right-handed pitcher). This engages your hips, adding power to your delivery. Pay particular attention to firing your post leg in and forward so that you finish the pitch strongly.

Location, Location, Location

Your first priority with the fastball—with any pitch—is to locate the ball where you want it. Occasionally that will be right over the middle of the plate, but most often it will be to the corners of the plate, where the batter can't get the sweet spot of the bat on the ball. Any pitcher with decent mechanics and good hand-eye coordination can improve his ability to locate his fastball—and he *must* do that. Through the years I've discovered that young pitchers show much better command of their fastball when you ask them to throw it to very precise locations. There are four major locations for throwing the fastball.

Down and over the Plate

This is your best "strike one" pitch. Aim over the middle of the plate, knee-high. This is a good way to begin any pitch sequence. If the batter takes the pitch, it's strike one. If he swings, he'll most likely hit a ground ball, and you have a chance for a one-pitch out. To produce a low strike, keep your fingers on top of the ball, avoid rushing your upper body forward, and strongly finish your pitch. Think about throwing the pitch downhill—on a downward angle to the plate.

Working ahead in the count allows you to control the at-bat.

> *If I'm facing a fastball hitter, I'm certainly not going to back down from throwing my best pitch. I mean, I have two different fast-balls—a four-seam and a two-seam—that I can throw to different locations. So you can say it's power against power, but I still feel like I own an advantage over the hitter because I can throw the ball where I want.*
>
> —Roger Clemens, four-time Cy Young Award winner

Up and over the Plate

Locating your fastball up and over the plate can be dangerous, to be sure. A good fastball hitter can hit this pitch a long way. But most hitters can't get on top of this pitch: they'll either swing and miss it or pop it into the air, especially if the pitch is thrown with good velocity. Power pitchers should use this location frequently, and it doesn't have to be thrown for a strike. If you're a control pitcher with only modest velocity, you should still pitch up in the zone—occasionally and with a purpose.

For example, suppose you're working a hitter down and away all day, and you see that he's beginning to make an adjustment to better cover that location. That would be a good time to throw a high, hard one, to adjust his eyes and to remind him that you can pitch to any location. Another good time to pitch up and over the plate is when you have seen a particular batter swing and miss at some borderline-high fastballs. Why not throw one a little higher and out of the strike zone? This is called "climbing the ladder," and it's a technique often used by major leaguers. You can also set up your change-up or other off-speed pitches by throwing a high fastball. You get the batter thinking "hard and up," then you throw something slow and down.

Low and Away

This is your bread-and-butter pitch once you've gotten ahead in the count. You want to hit the outer third of the plate, knee-high. Since this pitch is farthest from the batter's eyes, it's the toughest for him to judge. Even the very best hitters have trouble doing anything with this pitch. Remember what the hitters want—to drive the ball for distance. That's a tough chore when the pitch is a low-and-away strike. You'll get a lot of called strikes with this pitch, too, especially if you can prove to the umpire that you can consistently locate the ball there. Also, you'll generate some really weak swings, resulting in rollover ground balls and weak pop-ups to the opposite field. One caution: there is no place in baseball for high, outside fastballs. You may get away with it most of the time in Little League, but as you move to higher levels of baseball, this pitch gets hit hard and far. If you're pitching away, you must keep the ball down.

A strike on the outside part of the plate is usually the most difficult pitch for hitters to handle.

You can also use the low-and-away fastball to set up a pitch up and in to the batter. Make it your goal to dominate the low, outside part of the strike zone. *Any pitcher at any level of baseball who can routinely hit the low, outside part of the strike zone will be successful.*

> *The wildest pitch is not necessarily the one that goes back to the screen. It can also be the one that goes right down the middle.*
> —Sandy Koufax, Hall of Fame pitcher

Up and In

Notice that I didn't say "down and in." As you move to higher levels of baseball, you'll find that down and inside is no place for a fastball. It's too easy for the batter to simply drop his barrel on that pitch and drive it hard and for distance. If you're coming inside, you want the pitch to be at least as high as just beneath the batter's hands.

You pitch inside to keep the hitter honest. You get him out by pitching away, to your bread-and-butter location. And you don't have to pitch inside for a strike. Pitch the ball just off the inside corner, to a position that makes the hitter move his feet. You don't want to hit him, just to make him move his feet, to make him uncomfortable. Nobody likes to have a fastball whizzing past just a few inches away. If the batter swings, he will be jammed, hitting the ball off the handle of the bat, where he is unlikely to generate any power. Power pitchers may intimidate hitters by pitching in, but control pitchers need to pitch inside, too. Remember, you must use the entire width of the plate to be successful. Don't be afraid to pitch inside.

An occasional fastball thrown inside and high will make your other pitches and pitch locations more effective.

Making It Move

There are three major directions in which you can make your fastball move—in, out, and down. The best pitchers, such as Greg Maddux, know how to do all three. But even if you can't learn to make it move like Maddux, you must make every effort to create movement on your fastball: it's much more difficult for the batter to make good contact with a pitch that's sinking, tailing, or cutting than it is to hit a straight fastball.

As noted earlier in this chapter, movement is largely a product of how you grip and release the ball. We've already covered the various fastball grips and when and how to throw those pitches. Now, let's cover the special benefits of these moving fastballs and the strategic and tactical use of them.

When Is a Strike a Ball and a Ball a Strike?

The most obvious and important benefit of movement is that you get batters to swing at pitches that appear to be strikes but are really balls. A less obvious but equally important benefit is that they will not swing at pitches that appear to be balls but are really strikes.

Let's look at how this works. Suppose, for example, you're a right-handed pitcher facing a right-handed hitter. You decide to throw him a two-seam, tailing fastball. You start the pitch at the inner half of the plate. The batter sees it as a good pitch to hit and starts his swing. But the movement of the pitch, tailing hard toward the batter, takes the ball from the inner half of the plate to just out of the strike zone. (Yes, young pitchers can and do create this much movement!) Now the batter has very little chance of making solid contact with the ball. If he does make contact, he will most likely pull the ball foul—a strike for you. What you have done is made a ball look like a strike. The other part of this pitching secret is much harder to accomplish.

Using movement on your fastball to make a strike look like a ball is not easy, because for younger pitchers it most often involves throwing a pitch away from your arm side and trying to make it tail. But I have worked with young pitchers who can do it. What an advantage they have! To accomplish that sort of movement takes much practice and determination. Maybe they'll get it; maybe they won't. But it can't hurt to try.

> *The secret to pitching is to make your strikes look like balls and your balls look like strikes.*
>
> —Greg Maddux, four-time Cy Young Award winner

No matter how hard you throw, hitters will eventually catch up to straight fastballs delivered down the heart of the plate. Movement and pitch location are essential to becoming a successful pitcher at higher levels.

> *You gotta keep the ball off the fat part of the bat.*
> —Satchel Paige, Hall of Fame pitcher

Here's an example of when you would use such a pitch: Suppose you're a right-handed pitcher facing a right-handed power hitter who can drive the ball with power to all fields. Normally you would pitch around him, but the situation dictates that you must get him out. You decide to throw him a two-seam, tailing fastball that you start outside, off the plate. The pitch appears to the batter as though it will be a ball, outside by three or four inches, so he doesn't swing. The tailing action of the pitch, however, moves it back over the outside corner of the plate—a strike for you. This technique can also be used against a left-handed hitter. You throw the tailing fastball off the inside corner, starting out as a ball, and it tails back and catches the corner. You have made a strike look like a ball; when you can do that, you have become a real pitcher.

The Right Contact

Pitchers should be taught to covet contact, to want the batter to swing and put the ball in play. Remember, we want the right kind of contact, preferably something away from the sweet spot of the bat. That's where movement comes in.

A tailing fastball (see "The Two-Seam Fastball") thrown to a same-handed hitter (righty to righty, lefty to lefty) is designed to bore into the hitter, forcing him to hit the ball below the center of the bat barrel. Balls hit on that part of the bat don't go very far. Conversely, tailing fastballs thrown to opposite-hand hitters (righty to lefty, lefty to righty) are designed to move away from the hitter, forcing the batter to hit the ball off the end of the bat. Again, balls hit off the end of the bat don't go very far.

57

A cut fastball (see "The Cut Fastball") is mostly used against opposite-handed hitters. You start the pitch over the plate, and the cutting action makes the ball bore into the hitter, ideally forcing him to strike the ball below the barrel of the bat, jamming himself.

By design, the sinking fastball (see "The Sinking Fastball") moves down as it enters the hitting zone. It can and should be used against any batter. The down action on the ball often gets the batter to hit the top of the ball. This less-than-ideal contact often produces an infield grounder. This is an effective pitch to use when you have a strong infield behind you, or if you have only modest velocity.

There is no pitch more important to your arsenal than "ol' number one."

> *If I tried to throw harder than I could, the ball went slower than it normally would.*
>
> —Tom Seaver, Hall of Fame pitcher

Velocity

Every young pitcher wants to throw the ball harder. A high-velocity fastball is manly, something to make you the envy of your peers. And better velocity is a good thing, a worthwhile goal, providing that it isn't added at the expense of location or movement. How, then, can you improve the velocity of your fastball?

We've already covered two of the most important factors in generating maximum velocity: A good grip on the ball—firm, but tension free—and solid mechanics. A third element is a well-planned, ambitious throwing program that will make your arm healthier and stronger.

Building Arm Strength

Many young pitchers don't throw the ball enough to build good arm strength, to gain velocity the natural way. Arm soreness is more often the product of too little throwing rather than too much. I believe, as does Atlanta Braves pitching coach Leo Mazzone, that all pitchers—from Little League to the major leagues—should throw more often. The key is to throw often, but with *less than maximum exertion*. That means playing catch, long tossing (playing catch at greater distances than normal), and throwing "sides," which are focused sessions in the bullpen. You should be throwing a baseball every day—at less than full exertion. Throwing will not only increase your arm strength, it will help you to remain free of injury.

> *Always have the baseball in your hand, and always be throwing it. You'd be amazed how a simple thing like playing catch, back and forth, at a young age is a very useful way to build up arm strength and teach yourself about your natural mechanics. As a rule of thumb you don't want to overexert your arm when you throw the ball back and forth. But you will crank it up a bit to prepare for your next start.*
>
> —Leo Mazzone, Atlanta Braves pitching coach

Most Little League pitchers also play another position. Their throwing program will not affect their ability to play another position on the days they do not pitch. Remember, you build arm strength by throwing the ball.

Conditioning

Conditioning also plays a part in building velocity. The pitching delivery involves upper-body (torso) rotation around a strong, firm base (legs). Build up your legs with running—short sprints and long, slow jogs—and your upper body with very light weights and plenty of abdominal exercises—sit-ups, for example. And every part of your body should be flexible, so you'll need to do plenty of stretching. Chapter 8 provides specific exercises for adding flexibility, endurance, and strength.

The Psychology of Velocity

Throwing the fastball hard isn't just a physical act. There is a significant mental component, too. To throw the ball hard, you have to *want to* throw the ball hard. Part of throwing hard is the desire and ability to move your throwing arm and hand faster to, through, and beyond the release point.

A radar gun measures the velocity of the pitch the instant it leaves the pitcher's hand, so if the gun registers a pitch at 80 miles per hour, then the pitcher's hand was traveling at 80 miles per hour when the pitch was released. If the pitcher can increase his arm and hand speed to 82 miles per hour, his fastball will travel at 82 miles per hour. Why, then, do I see so many young pitchers who possess beautiful balance and mechanics and arm strength swing their arms and hands so slowly? I believe they fail to realize this simple fact of physics: arm and hand speed equals pitch speed.

You have to think aggressively, want to make your arm and hand move faster. Do this by first relaxing your wrist and forearm during the backswing, then focus on accelerating the hand and arm during the forward swing. Here's a drill that will help you increase your hand speed.

Hand-Speed Drill

Stand with your feet a little more than shoulder-width apart and about 35 feet from your throwing partner. Hold the ball in your glove at about chest level. Rotate your upper body—no leg movement—until your lead shoulder is parallel to the line of the pitch. Your throwing arm swings to the high-cocked, power position. Now, throw the ball to your partner, accelerating your throwing arm and hand as fast as you can and extending into a full finish position. The beauty of this drill is that because you get no benefit of leg power, you really feel the need to move your arm and hand fast to get anything on the ball. You should perform this drill at least three times per week.

Don't count on throwing harder just because you get older or bigger. Go out and work on getting that extra few miles per hour on your fastball.

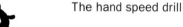
The hand speed drill

Changing Speeds with Your Fastball

You shouldn't only think about increasing the velocity of your fast-ball. You should also think about varying the velocity of your fast-ball. You will learn a change-up at some point, and the first step toward mastering that pitch is to learn how to change speeds with your fastball.

The easiest method of varying the speed of your fastball is to throw what pitchers call a "BP fastball." The initials BP stand for batting practice. So a BP fastball is one that is thrown at the same speed as a batting practice fastball, or somewhat slower than a game fastball. You don't change your mechanics to throw a BP fastball; you simply don't throw it quite as hard. If you can slow the speed just a few miles per hour, you will successfully disrupt the batter's timing—he'll be out in front of the pitch. And, later, when you go back to your hardest fastball, the batter may be just a little late.

Another way of changing speeds with your fastball is to use different grips. Remember, the four-seam grip will produce the greatest velocity. Any other grip—the two-seam, for example—will be a few miles per hour slower. Throwing two different fastballs to the same batter will not only give him a different look in terms of movement, but he'll be forced to adjust to a change of speed, too.

The bottom line on the fastball is this: You cannot win without a good one. They don't call the fastball the "ol' number one" for no reason. It comes first!

When throwing a fastball, understand that sometimes less is more. That means that by putting forth less effort, you're allowing your body to stay in balance and in rhythm and execute the proper mechanics (see next page).

Pitchers often make the mistake of trying to exert too much effort, which actually decreases the velocity of their pitches. Problems such as tension, tilting, rushing, or opening the front shoulder too quickly can corrupt your delivery. Stay smooth and focused (as shown here) and reap the benefits.

4

THE CHANGE-UP

The fastball is the most valuable and important pitch in baseball. The second most important and valuable pitch is the change-up, and it is definitely the second pitch you should learn and command.

The change-up is the companion pitch to the fastball. The change-up looks like a fastball but travels at a slower speed. It is thrown with the same technique, same spin, and same arm speed as the fastball. It is really little more than a fastball with a different grip.

Since the fastball is the most common pitch (and the one hitters most want to swing at), having a change-up provides you with many benefits. Here is a list of good things that come with the change-up:

- The change-up upsets the timing of the batter. Will your next pitch be slow or fast? It's very difficult to make solid contact when the velocity of the pitches is not consistent.
- The change-up establishes a third dimension to the strike zone: forward and back. You are pulling the hitter forward (with the change-up) and pushing him back (with the fastball). The hitter now has to defend not only the width and height of the

strike zone, but also the front and back. That's a tough chore for even the best hitter.

- Having a good change-up makes your fastball look faster. Seeing a few 50-mile-per-hour change-ups makes a 60-mile-per-hour fastball look fast. This is especially beneficial for pitchers who don't yet possess an overpowering fastball. Are you gaining real velocity? No. However, the hitter's perception is all you should care about.

- Your change-up will help you produce weak swings and weak contact. We throw a change-up not to get a called strike, but to get the hitter to swing. If you throw the change-up well, you'll get weak swings and weakly hit balls.

- The change-up has a psychological impact on hitters. Fool them once and they'll never forget. Hitters hate to be made to look bad, especially by a slow pitch. The change-up will always be in their minds, a distraction that may allow you to beat them with your fastball.

Qualities of a Good Change-Up

There is no question that adding a change-up to your arsenal will make you a more effective pitcher, but only if the change-up is a good one. As you develop the pitch, here are the qualities that you're striving for:

- The change-up must have the same spin as your fastball. Remember, you're trying to make the hitter think the pitch is a fastball, so it had better look like one.

> *Hitting is timing. Pitching is upsetting timing.*
> —Warren Spahn, Hall of Fame pitcher

- You must throw the change-up with fastball arm speed. You won't fool the batter by slowing down your arm. (Slowing your arm speed will also make it very difficult to control the change-up.) The hitter sees fastball arm speed and he thinks he's getting a fastball.

- The pitch must be located down in the strike zone, or even low and out of the strike zone. The further the pitch is from the batter's eyes, the more difficult for him to detect the change in velocity. Also, you want him to swing at the pitch, and it's harder for him to make good contact on pitches located at the bottom of the strike zone.

- You must throw your change-up over the plate. Don't be too "fine" by trying to hit the corners with this pitch. You can throw the most technically beautiful change-up that finishes just inches off the plate and the hitter won't swing, because he sees the pitch as a fastball for a ball! Make the batter believe the pitch is a *fastball for a strike.*

- Once you establish control of your change-up, you should try to make the pitch move. That is, try to make your change-up tail or sink. The change-up is a particularly effective pitch against opposite-handed hitters (e.g., right-handed pitcher vs. left-handed hitter). Having the ability to make the ball move away from the hitter makes the pitch more effective.

- The change-up should be approximately 10–12 miles per hour slower than your fastball. Too little difference in speed and the batter won't be fooled. Too much difference in speed and the batter has a chance to recognize the pitch and hit it hard.

Who Should Throw the Change-Up

I believe that every pitcher, from the Little League player to the top pitchers in professional baseball, should feature a change-up. Let's

LONG TOSS AND THE CHANGE-UP

Coaches are constantly after their pitchers to use long toss—playing catch at increasingly longer distances—to build arm strength. Long toss, though, is good for more than building arm strength; it's good for building that fastball arm speed you want for your change-up. The next time you go out to play long toss, use your change-up grip. At distances of 50–70 feet you'll find that you need fastball arm speed in order to reach your partner. You'll be building the confidence you need to swing your arm fast when you deliver your change-up. As a bonus, you'll be building arm strength, too.

To develop comfort throwing a change-up, use a change-up grip whenever you're playing catch.

examine, though, how very specific types of pitchers would bene-fit from a good change-up.

Power Pitcher

If you're a pitcher who routinely blows his fastball past hitters, who racks up high strikeout totals, who strikes fear into hitters with the speed of his pitches, then you are considered a "power pitcher." You are the type of pitcher who forces batters to make an adjust-ment to catch up to your fastball, because of its high velocity. How do batters adjust to you? They simply start their swings earlier. This is a simple adjustment for a good hitter to make, and pretty soon he'll be on your fastball, so you'll have to make an adjustment. That's when the change-up comes in handy. Then they can't sim-ply guess "fastball" without subjecting themselves to looking silly when you change speeds.

Finesse Pitcher

If you are a pitcher who does not possess an overpowering fastball, but gets hitters out because of precise location, then you are con-sidered a "finesse pitcher." You are the type of pitcher who con-founds hitters by working all areas of the strike zone (in, out, up, down) with no discernible pattern. Batters feel comfortable against you, because they know you can't throw the ball past them. Gen-erally, the hitter's approach against you is to look for a fastball that he can pull. When you make a mistake by locating your fastball too much over the middle of the plate, the hitter is right on the pitch; he hits it hard. You need a good change-up to disrupt the timing of the hitter.

A good change-up, one that forces hitters to be a little more hon-est in their approach, will make your fastball look faster. By chang-ing speeds, you're getting the hitters "in between." That is, they aren't sure whether to attack your fastball (go forward) or wait on your change-up (stay back). When they look for the change-up, your fastball appears to get to them more quickly. Where once they would have been right on your fastball, now they may be a little late with their swing. What once was a double in the gap may now be a simple pop fly. It is true that your fastball is "faster" only in the hitter's perception, but that's all that matters.

Gripping the Change-Up

Show me ten college pitchers and I'll show you ten different change-up grips, and that's fine. Those grips were developed over many years of trial and error. For young pitchers, though, many change-up grips are not possible. Younger pitchers often have small hands and fingers and can only manage certain grips. For example, a young pitcher should not attempt any pitch that requires him to have much of his palm in contact with the ball. He simply doesn't have the requisite experience or feel to accurately throw such a

The four-seam circle change grip

pitch. Whichever grip he chooses, he must develop complete trust in that grip.

The Circle Change-Up

The circle change-up is probably the most popular change-up. It's so called because the grip requires you to make a circle by bending your index finger down to meet your thumb. There are two popular varieties of the circle change-up. Which one you should use depends largely on what type of fastball you throw.

The four-seam circle change-up. If you normally throw a four-seam fastball, you should try the four-seam circle change-up, because you want both pitches to spin in precisely the same way. To throw this pitch, you place the pads of your middle and ring fingers across the seam of the ball and approximately an inch apart. Hold the ball deep in these fingers, but don't squeeze it. Slide your pinky finger underneath the ball. (Your pinky and thumb are used to keep the ball off your palm.) Move your thumb to the inside of the baseball and bend your index finger down to meet your thumb, forming a circle.

The two-seam circle change-up. If you normally throw a two-seam fastball, you should use the two-seam circle change-up, because, again, you want the two pitches to have the same spin. Your thumb, index finger, and pinky finger perform the same functions as with the four-seam circle change-up. This grip differs only in that your middle finger and ring finger are placed on the seam where it runs closest together. Much as with the two-seam fastball, the two-seam circle change, when thrown properly, will tail or sink away from an opposite-hand batter.

Important note: Because of varying hand sizes, not all young pitchers will be able to perfectly grip the circle change-up. You may not be able to locate your pinky finger in the ideal position, and the

The two-seam circle change grip

A frequent mistake made by pitchers attempting to throw a change-up is gripping the ball deep in their palm.

circle formed by your index finger and thumb may not be perfect, either. That's all right. What's most important is that you hold the ball deep in your fingers with minimal palm contact. Throw the ball with your fingers, not your palm.

> *I went from experimenting with [the change-up] to being confident enough to throw it with the bases loaded and a full count in the World Series.*
>
> —Tom Glavine, major league pitcher

The Batting Practice Fastball

If your hand size won't allow you to throw a circle change-up, or if you can't seem to master the pitch, you can still change speeds. Simply throw two different fastballs, one at your normal velocity and one where you take a little speed off. The latter is known as a batting practice (BP) fastball (see Chapter 3). The pitch won't be quite as deceptive as a change-up, because you will have slower arm speed than with your normal fastball. Still, it can throw a hitter's timing off just enough so that he loses some of his power.

Throwing the Change-Up

Throwing a change-up is no different from throwing a fastball. Your technique should be the same: good arm speed, good extension, with a full finish. Young pitchers, though, make all sorts of changes to their delivery when throwing the change-up, because they don't trust the grip, which is so radically different from what they are accustomed to. The Golden Rule for throwing the change-up: *trust your grip!* The grip will do all the work for you. It is

MAKING YOUR GRIP

Observant hitters and coaches can sometimes detect what pitch is coming by how the pitcher grips the ball in his glove. For example, a pitcher who takes more than a second or two to "make" his grip by digging into his glove is probably throwing an off-speed pitch, maybe a change-up. This is especially true of young pitchers who are just learning the change-up and whose hand size doesn't allow them to grip the ball quickly. If you are one of these pitchers, consider beginning with the change-up grip before each pitch. You'll be able to easily move to your fastball grip, and throwing a change-up won't require any digging into your glove. The more practical, longer-lasting solution is to diligently work on making your change-up grip move seamlessly. Don't give the batter an edge by tipping off the type of pitch you're about to throw.

not possible to use the circle change-up grip and throw a baseball at the same velocity as you can with any of the common fastball grips.

Maintain Arm Speed

You cannot throw an effective change-up if you slow your arm down. You must move your arm and hand at the same speed as you do when you throw your fastball. If you try to slow the

Throwing the inside of the ball will produce sinking and/or tailing action on your change-up.

pitch down by slowing your arm speed or contorting your body (e.g., dragging your pivot foot), the batter will notice and the pitch won't be effective. Trust the grip and throw the pitch just like your fastball.

> *The goal is to maintain arm speed. Arm speed promotes deception. Deception gets the hitter out.*
>
> —Leo Mazzone, major league pitching coach

To Slow It Down and Make It Move

76

If you feel that the speed differential between your fastball and change-up is not sufficient, you'll want to slow your change-up down. First, check your grip to make certain that the ball is being held deep in your fingers. Second, make sure that as you throw the pitch, you stay "inside the ball," which means that even though your index finger isn't helping to grip the ball, it must still be active during the release phase. You want to be throwing the side of the ball closest to your body.

Throwing the circle. One way of staying inside the ball is to imagine that the circle formed by your index finger and thumb is a ball. When you release the pitch, think of throwing this imaginary ball. This is referred to as "throwing the circle." The extra pronation of the wrist created by throwing the circle will slow the pitch down. As a bonus, you may also generate movement by staying inside the ball. For a right-handed pitcher, the ball will move down and away from a left-handed batter.

Locating the Change-Up

You should always try to locate your change-up down and over the plate. Your target is an area from the bottom of the strike zone to the ground and anywhere over the plate. Once you have become proficient with the pitch, you may want to try locating on the outer part of the plate rather than the inner half. But at first, anywhere over the plate will do.

One thought some pitchers use is to try to throw the change-up between their catcher's feet.

Down

You want the ball down because the farther the pitch is from the hitter's eyes, the more difficult it will be for him to detect the change of speed. Also, keeping the ball down makes it more difficult for the batter to hit the ball with any power.

Over the Plate

You want the ball over the plate because you want the batter to swing. You can throw the most beautiful change-up that is just off the plate and the batter won't swing, because he saw the pitch as a fastball for a ball. You don't throw the change-up to get a called strike; you want the batter to swing and make weak contact.

When and When Not to Use the Change-Up

Unlike the fastball, the pitch for any hitter and any time, the change-up should be used in more discriminating fashion. There

Because hitters have trouble identifying the change-up, they often get out on their front foot and have only their arms left to swing the bat.

are very specific hitters and situations when the change-up is your best option, and when it's your worst option.

Best Times

- Against a hitter who has quality bat speed and proven ability to pull your fastball
- Against a hitter who strides open (in the bucket)
- Against any hitter whose upper body moves forward too aggressively during his stride (drifting)
- Against hitters who only use the pull side of the field
- Against a first-pitch swinger who has seen your fastball in at least one earlier at-bat
- When you are behind in the count against a good fastball hitter, particularly if first base is not occupied

Worst Times

- Against any hitter who has trouble handling your fastball
- Before a hitter has had a chance to see your fastball
- As a two-strike pitch against a contact hitter who uses the entire field
- Against a same-handed hitter who exclusively uses the opposite field

You should not begin using your change-up in game situations until you can successfully throw it seven out of ten times in the bullpen. Be smart when you use the pitch in a game for the first time. Pick spots where the pitch can't hurt you, perhaps in a game in which you have a comfortable lead or against a hitter who won't

A change-up down in the strike zone will generally produce weakly hit ground balls.

hurt you with the long ball. Track the results of the pitch. Once you see that the pitch works, your confidence will soar.

Remember, the change-up is a great pitch, an excellent companion to your fastball. However, it is no substitute for your fastball. Don't go overboard by trying to make hitters look foolish; get the hitters out with your fastball whenever you can.

CHANGE-UP DAY

On our college team we have a rule that our pitchers devote one day a week to the change-up. We call it Change-Up Day. From the beginning to the end of practice, the pitchers throw only change-ups. All of the warm-ups, drills, long toss, and bullpen sessions are change-ups only. This is designed to build trust in the grip and confidence in the pitch. It doesn't take long for the pitchers to begin believing in the efficacy of the change-up.

5

THE CURVEBALL

Should Little League pitchers throw curveballs? This is one of the most commonly asked questions posed by parents, coaches, and even the players themselves. To throw the curve or not to throw the curve has been a topic of debate for decades. There is no simple answer. My position is this: you don't need a curveball to be successful in Little League competition, so you shouldn't throw one. Learn how to get the batters out with your fastball, and if you want to change speeds, use your change-up.

Many young pitchers already do throw curveballs, and many throw them well. Many more young pitchers will begin throwing curveballs despite protestations from me and others. The important thing, then, is to learn to properly throw the curveball and to be judicious in its use.

I believe that when thrown properly the curveball is no more injurious to the arm than any other pitch. Young pitchers may injure themselves when their curveball technique is faulty. The main problem with learning the curveball is that it is a "feel" pitch that also requires you to turn your wrist in a manner completely different from when you throw the fastball or change-up. That is, it requires you to put feel and touch on the pitch, while at the same time turning your wrist in a completely unfamiliar fashion. Feel pitches

require much repetitious practice. Trial and error under the supervision of a knowledgeable coach is the way to learn. Before you decide to master the curveball, be aware of this: it is the hardest pitch to learn and to teach. However, if you can learn the perfect curveball technique, it's an excellent addition to your arsenal of pitches. Here are some of the things that a good curveball will do for you:

- The curveball provides a change of speed off your fastball, so it upsets the hitter's timing.
- The curveball breaks in two planes, vertical and horizontal, so it's tough for the hitter to track. Any pitch that deviates from a straight line becomes much harder to hit.
- The curveball lands in a significantly different location from where it starts. Batters often swing at where a curveball starts, rather than where it will finish.
- The curveball can be a valuable strikeout pitch, one that makes the batter swing and miss.
- Against all but the very best hitters, the curveball allows you to shift your defense to the pull side of the field. It becomes very easy to predict where the hitters will hit the ball.
- The curveball keeps the hitters back, so that they can't be so aggressive against your fastball. This opens up the inner half of the plate for your fastball. The ideal way to pitch any hitter, even the very best, is to throw him hard pitches up and in and soft pitches low and away.
- The curveball has a psychological impact on hitters similar to that of a change-up. If you make a hitter look bad with something slow, he'll never forget. The curveball will remain forever etched on his brain. This makes your fastball seem faster and better.

Qualities of a Good Curveball

Now that you understand what a good curveball can do for you, let's examine exactly what constitutes a good curveball.

Showing the batter a breaking pitch makes your fastball more effective. A breaking ball away, followed by a fastball inside (shown here) often freezes hitters and earns a called strike.

84

- The curveball is thrown with maximum overspin. This is the opposite of the fastball, which is thrown with maximum backspin. You want to throw the curveball with "tight" rotation. That is, the hitter should see nothing but the red seam as the ball approaches. In fact, when you throw the curveball perfectly, the seam looks like a little red dot. The hitter cannot see the white part of the ball. The rotation makes the pitch look like a fastball.

BY ANY OTHER NAME

The vocabulary of baseball is full of wonderful nicknames. If you're going to play the game ("walk the walk"), you might as well be able to "talk the talk," too. Some nicknames are for players (the Yankee Clipper, the Bambino, the Big Hurt), some for batted balls (Baltimore chop, Texas Leaguer, a bomb), and some for pitches. The curveball has some especially entertaining nicknames: bender, deuce, hook, hammer, Uncle Charlie, drop, downer, and yakker. Also, if you have a sharp break on your curveball, you might say that it "bites," "growls," "chews," or "hisses."

- The curveball should be located near the bottom of the strike zone, preferably from the middle of the plate to the outside corner. This takes away the hitter's power and increases the chance that he'll swing over the pitch. Remember, you have to prove that you can throw the curveball for strikes. Then, you can get the hitters to chase it out of the strike zone when you want them to. If you can't throw the curveball for a strike, the batters will ignore it and stay focused on your fastball.
- The ideal curveball breaks in two planes: down and across. This makes it very difficult for the batter to track. This break should occur because of the tight spin and velocity of the pitch, not because of gravity alone. If you can't make the ball break sharply, or "bite," then it's not a curveball; it's a "gravity pitch," which is quite easy for the hitters to track and hit hard.

Curveballs that break down in the strike zone often produce pop flies or weakly hit ground balls.

- The curveball should provide a good change of speed off your fastball. Ideally, the curveball should be approximately 12–15 miles per hour slower than your fastball.

Who Should Throw the Curveball

Not every young pitcher should even attempt to learn the curveball. Some pitchers who attempt the curveball are merely doing the batter a favor by throwing a slow pitch that does not bite and is easy to recognize as something other than a fastball. If you throw a curveball, pay attention to the feedback the hitters provide. If they hit it hard, or they ignore it and take the pitch for a ball, then you should assume that the pitch is not yet game-ready. If you haven't thrown a curveball in a game and are wondering if you should, there are three standards to consider. If you meet all three, then you are ready to throw the curveball in game competition.

Velocity

Do you throw the ball hard enough, with perfect spin, to get the sharp break you want from your curveball? Yes, velocity is important to the curveball, too. You need to throw the pitch hard enough to generate good rotation of the seam, so that the ball moves quickly off a straight line—it has bite. It is important to make the distinction between a sharp break and the ball dropping merely because of gravity.

Be honest with yourself. If your curveball doesn't have a good bite to it, then it probably won't fool good hitters. If you possess only a modest fastball by Little League standards, then your curveball probably isn't going to be your best choice for an off-speed pitch. Stick with the change-up.

Perfect Technique

Before you take the pitch into the game, you must perfect your technique to the satisfaction of your coach and parents. I've seen many young pitchers who can throw a curveball with good bite but whose technique was faulty to the point that I was concerned that continued use of the curveball might cause an arm injury. Perfect technique means that you will develop a good pitch and remain healthy, too. Trading a few outs for a sore arm doesn't make sense. Be patient.

Strikes

Even if you have the requisite arm strength and the right technique for the curveball, you'll still need to throw it for strikes for it to be an effective pitch. My standard is that you should be able to throw the pitch for a strike six or seven times out of ten during practice before you can use it in the game. Otherwise, why bother?

PRACTICE AT SHORT DISTANCE

One thing that all good curveballs have in common is tight, rapid rotation, or spin. You can't throw a hard-breaking curveball if you can't make the ball spin correctly. The best way to perfect the correct spin is to practice at short distance, perhaps 30–35 feet. This allows you to focus solely on the spin, without worrying about velocity or location. Once you can spin the ball correctly at short distances, then you can move back to the pitching mound.

The bottom line: if you have a strong arm and perfect technique, and you can consistently throw the curveball for strikes during practice, then you are ready to snap off a few during the game. Otherwise, stick with the fastball–change-up combination.

Gripping the Curveball

There are many ways to grip the curveball. I believe, however, that there is one *best* way: the four-seam grip. This grip affords the best chance at getting maximum spin on the ball; fast, tight rotation is what makes the ball break sharply. The four-seam grip also allows you to perfectly position your middle finger and thumb on the seam of the ball. These are your two most critical fingers for throwing a good curveball: your middle finger pulls and your thumb pushes.

To grip the curveball, find a wide gap between parts of the seam and place your middle finger along the inside of the right part of the seam (for a right-hander). You want to feel that you have "hooked" the seam. That is, you have leverage so that your middle finger can pull on the seam, thereby imparting overspin when you release the pitch.

Lay your index finger right next to your middle finger. Hold the ball securely (but not tightly) in your hand. Taking a grip with a gap between your hand and the ball, such as you do with the fastball, will require your fingers to work alone, and that won't allow you to spin the ball as rapidly as you want to. Holding the ball more securely in your hand means that your fingers, hand, wrist, and forearm will all be working together as one unit when you release the pitch.

Place your thumb underneath the ball, slightly bent and on the seam. You need to feel that your thumb can push on the seam, helping your middle finger impart overspin on the ball. The inside of your ring finger rests against the outside of the ball. Again, you

Grip the curveball by placing your middle finger on the inside of the seam. Your middle finger pulls and your thumb pushes.

must grip the ball securely but not tightly. Your wrist and forearm should feel loose.

Throwing the Curveball

The release and finish of the curveball delivery are unique. Your wrist position at release and the completion of your forward armswing are different than with the fastball or change-up. The beginning of your forward armswing, though, should be identical to that of your other pitches.

Forward Armswing

As you begin your forward armswing to deliver a curveball, you should be thinking "fastball." By thinking fastball during the first

When throwing a curveball, turn your wrist inward just before you reach the point of release. Think "fastball" throughout your motion until just before you release the ball.

two-thirds of your prerelease armswing, you will keep from prematurely turning your wrist and releasing the curveball too early. Releasing the curveball too early most often results in a "hanging curveball," a pitch devoid of any good qualities, unless you're a hitter looking for something easy to hit.

I'll be working with a pitcher and tell him to throw the breaking ball slower but spin it faster, and all of a sudden—whoosh—he gets that sharp break.

—Leo Mazzone, major league pitching coach

Release

As you near your release point, turn your wrist so that your palm is facing your head. Your wrist must remain straight and relaxed. Bending or bowing your wrist so that your palm faces down toward the ground is dangerous. This is called "wrapping" and will adversely affect the pitch and may cause injury to your elbow.

As you release the ball, snap your wrist forward, pulling down on the seam with your middle finger and pushing up on the seam with your thumb. It's like snapping your fingers, only with a ball between them. The ball will rotate out of your hand with overspin, the exact opposite of the backspin that you generate when throwing a four-seam fastball. Whenever throwing the curveball, think "later release" rather than sooner.

When you throw the ball with perfect rotation, the batter and catcher don't see much white on the ball. They see only the red seam, and because the ball is rotating so perfectly, the seam blends together to create what appears to be a little red dot. When you can create the red dot, you know you are releasing and spinning the ball correctly.

Finish

The remainder of your forward armswing, the part that comes after release, is significantly different than that for the fastball. For example, you should never fully extend your elbow. Instead, it remains bent and is slightly "cushioned" in toward your body. Also, finish

Throw [the curveball] first before you turn it, and then watch it turn the corner and go down.

—Johnny Sain, major league pitcher and coach

with your palm toward the sky, with your thumb up—not toward the ground, as it would be with the fastball.

Locating the Curveball

It's safe to say that you always want to keep your curveball down rather than up. How far down depends upon your goal for the pitch, because there is more than one kind of curveball.

Get Me Over

The most common type of curveball is one that is thrown with the intent of being a strike. This is commonly referred to as a "get me over" curveball. You should locate this pitch somewhere around knee-high in the strike zone. When you are facing a same-handed hitter, you want to locate this pitch from the middle of the plate to the outside corner. It's all right to locate this pitch from the middle of the plate to the inside corner when facing an opposite-handed hitter. You must prove you can throw your curveball in the strike zone if you want the hitters to swing at it. Never intentionally locate your curveball higher in the strike zone, because the pitch becomes easy to identify and even easier to hit.

Strike 'Em Out

Your second curveball is one thrown with the intention of getting the batter to chase it out of the strike zone. It is a strikeout pitch generally thrown when you are ahead in the count. You

Your arm remains bent and is slightly "cushioned" in toward your body in the follow-through. Your palm faces the sky with your thumb pointed upward.

Curveballs thrown up in the strike zone are often hit a long way. High curveballs are often caused by trying to throw the pitch too hard.

throw the "strike 'em out" curveball so that it lands below the bottom of the strike zone, even if it means bouncing it in the dirt. This pitch is usually reserved for when you feel you have the batter set up for a curveball, or for when the batter has shown a weakness against your curveball, or for when there is a base open and you don't mind walking a hitter, perhaps on a 3–2 pitch.

You must practice this pitch, because it's not as easy as you think to intentionally throw your curveball down in the dirt. To get your

You get ahead [of the hitters] with strikes, and you get them out with balls.

—Larry Andersen, major league pitcher

curveball down and out of the strike zone, try shortening your glide step. This gets your hand more on top of the ball, making it easier to throw a low pitch. Remember, when batters fall behind in the count, they tend to expand their strike zone, making it easier for you to get them to chase a bad pitch.

TRY THE BACK DOOR

Another pitch you can try is the so-called "back door" curveball. This is when you intentionally try to throw your curveball to the outside corner against an opposite-handed hitter. You start your curveball off the plate and hope to get enough horizontal movement on the pitch to catch the outside corner. It is a tough pitch to master but can be a great out pitch, too. The ball is never within the strike zone until the last moment.

One caution: never intentionally try to catch the inside corner with a curveball against a same-handed hitter. This is courting disaster, because the pitch starts and stays within the batter's power zone, and he won't need to execute a very good swing to hit the ball hard.

Common Flaws

Young pitchers make more mistakes throwing the curveball than any other pitch. Much of this is because the pitch requires a different grip, release, and finish than the fastball. Another major reason is the young pitcher's desire to make the ball break sharply and over great distances. All of these flaws in technique can be corrected—if you know what you're looking for. Here's a list of the most common curveball problems and the solutions:

- *You release the pitch too early.* This is often caused by turning the wrist too early, or by overthrowing the pitch. Think "later" rather than sooner, and remember that spin and location, not armspeed, are the most important ingredients of a good curveball.
- *Your wrist is wrapped at release.* At release, your wrist must be straight with your palm facing your head.
- *You are fully extending your elbow after your release.* Your elbow must remain slightly bent and more toward your body than with the fastball.
- *You are working your hand around the ball instead of over it.* This happens when pitchers focus too much on horizontal movement of the pitch rather than making the ball go down. Remember to pull down at release. Make the ball go down before you worry about any horizontal movement.

Common flaw: turning the wrist too early

Common flaw: wrapping your wrist at release

Common flaw: working around the ball

Common flaw: gripping the ball too much in your palm

Common flaw: gripping the ball too much in your fingers

- *Your glide step (stride) is too short.* A slightly shorter stride will help you get your fingers more on top of the ball, making it easier for you to get your curveball down in the strike zone. If you shorten your stride too much, however, you'll be throwing all your curveballs into the dirt.
- *You are slowing down your arm speed.* Velocity is important to the curveball. Try to throw the pitch hard. Batters will notice if you slow your arm down.
- *You are gripping the ball too much in your fingers.* Your fingers need help to generate the best rotation. Grip the ball with your hand, too. When you engage your hand in the grip, you get the strength of your fingers, hand, wrist, and forearm all working together.

When and When Not to Use the Curveball

As with the change-up, there are certain hitters and situations for which the curveball may be your best option, or your worst option. (Whenever you have serious doubt as to which pitch to throw, go with your fastball.) Use your curveball wisely and it will be a great pitch for you, one that sets batters up and gets them out. On the other hand, if you use your curveball foolishly or too much, you'll wish you never started throwing the pitch. As with anything, experience will be your best teacher. Here are some general guidelines for when to throw or not throw your curveball.

Best Times

- Against a dead-pull hitter
- Against a hitter who strides open (in the "bucket")
- Against a hitter who drifts to the ball (his upper body moves forward too soon)

LEAVE WELL ENOUGH ALONE

At every level of baseball—from Little League to the major leagues—pitchers have a tendency to follow a really good curveball with a really bad one. I believe this is because they try to make the second pitch better than the first. Trying to improve upon a good curve often results in overthrowing or some other breakdown in technique. This leads to a bad pitch, one that is at best a ball, or worse, one that gets hit a long way. If the first curveball is a good one, with a sharp break and located low in the strike zone, how do you throw a better one? You don't. You should simply relax and repeat the pitch. Pitching is like many other things in that it's sometimes best to leave well enough alone.

- Early in the count against a good fastball hitter
- Behind in the count to a good hitter with first base open
- Against a hitter who habitually swings at the first pitch
- Immediately after throwing a good fastball to the inside corner
- Immediately after throwing a good curveball

Worst Times
- Against any hitter who can't handle your fastball
- Against a contact hitter when you're ahead in the count
- Immediately after you've thrown a change-up
- Anytime you'd rather throw something else
- In any count in which you absolutely must have a strike (choose the fastball instead)

The Slider

The best advice I can offer for throwing a slider is—don't (at least not yet). The good news is that the slider is probably an easier pitch to learn than the curveball and it is easier to throw for strikes. The problems are that it is also easy to injure yourself with this pitch if your technique is faulty, and a poorly thrown slider is the easiest of all pitches to hit. I believe it is best to wait until your body is more fully developed before attempting to throw sliders, and this should only be done under the supervision of a knowledgeable coach. For now you can throw the cut fastball (see Chapter 3), which is similar in some ways to the slider, but without much of the danger.

6

PREPARATION, STRATEGY, AND TACTICS

I wish I had a dollar for every time I've heard a pitcher described as someone with a "million-dollar arm and a ten-cent head." What the critic is indelicately saying is that the pitcher's wonderful physical skills are being undone by a lack of good preparation and good thinking before and during the game. The pitcher has the talent to be successful, but his lack of planning and mental acuity is holding him back.

It's true: you pitch not just with your arm, but with your head, too. The good news is that you can develop into a thinking man's pitcher the same way you develop your mechanics and your pitches: by focused practice and paying attention to the nonphysical attributes that are part of the makeup of good pitchers. Here are some characteristics every coach would like to see in his pitchers:

- *Preparation.* You've done everything necessary to be ready for the task at hand.
- *Competitiveness.* You are determined to perform well and to win, regardless of the score, the opponent, or whether you have your best stuff that day.

- *Mental toughness.* You handle every situation—good or bad—with composure. Your focus is unwavering.
- *Positive attitude.* Your outlook and approach are always centered on the good and never on the bad.
- *Adaptability.* You are able to adjust to any unforeseen circumstances that arise.
- *Good teammate.* You show appreciation for your teammates' efforts, praising them when they do well and encouraging them even when they fail.

All of these traits factor into your game performance. If you possess enough of them in sufficient quantity and have physical talent, your coach will likely send you out to the mound on game day. You must have a well-developed plan for game day. Separate the day into four parts:

103

1. Pregame planning (including goal setting)
2. Pregame warm-up
3. The game
4. Postgame evaluation

Pregame Planning

You should begin every game day by constructing a plan for how you want the game to play out. This involves setting goals, making a scouting report on the opposition, reviewing your own strengths and weaknesses, and, finally, creating your mission statement.

Setting Goals

You must have goals. Setting goals helps you to direct your attention and focus toward achieving very specific tasks. Some goals are short-term, such as a 1-2-3 first inning, while others are long-term, such as pitching a complete-game shutout. Short-term goals help to keep us focused "in the moment," and long-term goals help us to sustain our efforts.

Set your goals high but understand that they are always subject to revision. Hall of Fame pitcher Sandy Koufax always had the same goal before every game: a perfect game. If Koufax walked a batter, he adjusted his goal to a no-hitter. If he allowed a hit, he set a new goal for a one-hit shutout, and so on. Whatever your personal goals, the first order of business is to win the game. Here is a sample list of game-day goals (in no particular order):

- Win the game
- Get as many one-pitch outs as possible (welcome contact)
- Allow no walks
- Establish command of my fastball
- Get them out 1-2-3 in the first inning and in any inning after my team scores
- Get ahead (in the count), and stay ahead
- Remember to be a good fielder, too
- Allow no runs

Remember that goals are important, that they can improve your performance, but that they are always subject to change. Failure to achieve a goal does not make you a failure: it means only that you need to adjust that goal for that day. Goal-setting pitchers are like United States Marines: they must be able to improvise, adapt, and overcome.

Opposition Scouting Report

Most Little League competition occurs within a league format. That is, you play the same teams several times during the season, giving you the advantage of having some familiarity with the opposing hitters. You can use this information about the hitters to develop a scouting report. This report is used to identify who is a power

Keeping a pitching chart can be very helpful, especially if you face a team a second time. It can act as your personal scouting report.

hitter, who bunts, who uses only the pull side of the field, who is the best fastball hitter, who can't handle your fastball, and so on. Once you have assessed and categorized the opposing hitters by their strengths and weaknesses, you should do a scouting report on yourself.

Personal Scouting Report

In order to determine precisely how to attack the opposing hitters, you must first make a review of your own strengths and weaknesses. Make a list of what you are good at and not so good at. Match up your list of strengths and weaknesses against those of your opponents.

Pay particular attention to any of your strengths that match a weakness of an opposing hitter. For example, if one of your strengths is the ability to locate your fastball on the outside corner, and two of their hitters cannot handle fastballs away, then you know how to attack them. Also pay attention to any of your strengths that match an opposing hitter's strength. Suppose you are a fastball pitcher and three guys in their lineup are good fastball hitters. Does this mean that you shouldn't throw them the fastball? No! You should never abandon your strength. However, you must understand the need to properly locate your fastball—in, out, up, down—against these good fastball hitters.

Another possibility is when an opponent's weakness matches your weakness (e.g., a bad off-speed hitter vs. a bad off-speed pitcher). This is a difficult situation. You should show him the pitch he struggles with, perhaps early in the count. When it comes time to get him out, though, you should go with your strength.

Below are scouting reports and plans of attack for two hitters:

Jamal Johnson: Right-handed hitter. He makes consistent contact but with little power. Jamal is a very selective hitter who rarely swings until he has a strike in the count. He uses the entire field. Jamal is a tough out. Plan of attack: go right after him with my fastball. Get ahead in the count and make him hit the ball.

Kevin MacDonald: Left-handed hitter. Kevin is a powerful hitter who rarely hits a ball to the left side of the field—a dead-pull hitter. He likes the fastball from the middle of the plate to the inside corner. He is not very good against off-speed pitches. Kevin is a dangerous hitter but can be pitched to. Plan of attack: when there are no runners on base, I will attack early with fastballs on the outside part of the plate, then finish him with change-ups and curveballs. If there are runners on base, I will not give him a fastball to hit.

Mission Statement

While your opposition and personal scouting reports lead you to conclusions about how to attack specific hitters, you must still complete a more general plan for the game. This is your mission state-

PLAN B

Sometimes the best-made plans of pitchers become impossible to execute. Inevitably there will be a game when you don't have command of a certain pitch, or your velocity isn't what it normally is, or your original plan just isn't working. That's when it's important to have a backup plan, a Plan B.

For example, if your change-up isn't working, your Plan B may call for you to throw more curveballs as your off-speed pitch, or to selectively throw the change-up to merely remind the batter that you have one. If you are a power pitcher with a big-time fastball, you will eventually have a game during which you don't have your best velocity. Your Plan B calls for better location—hitting the corners—and for more frequent use of your off-speed pitches. A pitcher who knows only one way to pitch is going to have some rough days. Having a Plan B to fall back on gives you a chance for success even on days when you aren't at your best.

107

ment, which includes a listing of imperatives that you believe in and adhere to, regardless of the opposition. Unlike goals, which may change from game to game and are always subject to revision, your mission statement remains a constant. The following items should be included in every pitcher's mission statement:

- I will establish command of my fastball.
- I will relentlessly attack the strike zone.
- I welcome contact.
- I will use my off-speed pitches intelligently and judiciously.
- I will work fast.
- I will remain positive regardless of the situation.

Warming Up

Your pregame warm-up session must involve more than walking down to the bullpen and throwing a couple of dozen pitches. Warming up includes running, stretching, planning, throwing, and evaluating. All of this should be done as part of a well-developed, consistent routine. Your routine is subject to change, of course, depending upon how well it prepares you for the game.

Running

You should always run as the first part of your warm-up routine. Running should be in the form of a brief jog, perhaps two minutes in duration. Running will warm your muscles and get your blood flowing. (You never want to stretch cold muscles.) Many pitchers jog from foul pole to foul pole. Do this twice and you're ready for the next stage of your warm-up.

Stretching

Once you've warmed up your muscles, take a few minutes to stretch them. Stretch each muscle until you feel some slight discomfort, and then hold the stretch a few seconds longer. Work from the ground up, stretching your legs first, then your hips, back, side, hands, arms, shoulder, and neck. (See Chapter 8 for detailed illustrated descriptions of how to stretch your muscles.) After stretching, you are ready to begin the throwing stage of your warm-up.

Throwing

Begin by tossing the ball lightly with your catcher—on flat ground—at a distance of 35–40 feet. After ten throws, move back to 45 feet (ten throws), then to 50 feet (ten throws), then to 60 feet (five throws). As you move back, you should begin adding more velocity to your throws, so that your last few are close to full speed. Now you are ready to step onto the mound.

Begin loosening up by throwing from flat ground at a shortened distance.

Warm-up pitches. Here are some general guidelines for your pregame warm-up pitches:

- Throw a high percentage of fastballs (at least 70 percent).
- Begin and end with the fastball.
- Throw all but the last few pitches at less than maximum exertion.
- Always throw to a very precise location.
- Throw no more than 35–40 pitches.
- Pause for a few seconds between pitches.

The following is a sample bullpen warm-up:

Four fastballs to the low center of the strike zone
Two fastballs to the outside corner
Two fastballs to the inside corner
Four change-ups
Four fastballs to the low center of the strike zone
Two fastballs to the outside corner
Two fastballs to the inside corner
Four curveballs
Four fastballs to the low center of the strike zone
Fastball to the inside corner
Curveball
Fastball to the outside corner
Change-up
Fastball to the inside corner
Curveball
Fastball to the outside corner
Change-up
Four fastballs to the low center of the strike zone (thrown at
    game speed)
Total: 40 pitches (28 fastballs, 6 change-ups, 6 curveballs)

As a starting pitcher, don't complete your pregame routine and walk directly to the mound. Plan your time so that you can rest for

Pitchers should concentrate more on locating pitches during their bullpens. First of all, I throw 99 percent fastballs in the bullpen because no one has ever had success without command of their fastball.

—Curt Schilling, major league pitcher

a few minutes before you have to go to the mound. You'll get an opportunity to throw up to eight pitches from the mound before facing the first batter.

The Game

You're preparing to face your first batter of the day. It is time to take your mind and your arm into battle. Your first order of business is to get your mind into the right state.

Power of Positive Thinking

Tell yourself that regardless of what happens today, good or bad, you will remain in a positive frame of mind. You will consistently focus on what you need to do and how to do it, and then let your talent and training take over. You are prepared. You can do this!

Visualize a positive result and then simply execute.

Visualization

This is a picture in your mind's eye of positive actions from the past. It is a mental rehearsal for a future act. You can see yourself painting the outside corner with your fastball, because you've done it so many times in the past. You can see yourself retiring a particular hitter because you've done it before. If you can see it, you can do it.

Tactical Thinking

As the game unfolds, situations will present themselves requiring you to make quick, tactical decisions. You have to be able to adapt, improvise, and overcome. You may even have to deviate from your overall strategy. You must keep your eyes and mind open so that you can gather all the information available that will determine your decision making.

Reading the Batter

How do you know where to pitch to a particular hitter? Much can be gained from remembering how you got him out in the past, or how you didn't get him out. But suppose you've never seen a hitter before; how do you know how and where to pitch him?

One way is to "read" the batter. That is, use your powers of observation to learn his stance, the way he holds the bat, his stride, his swing, and even how he takes a pitch. Here are some things to look for:

- A batter who starts from an open stance—left foot toward the third base line (for a right-handed hitter)—may be vulnerable to pitches on the outer part of the plate.
- A batter who starts from a closed stance—his left foot is closer to the plate than his right foot (for a right-handed batter)—may be vulnerable to pitches on the inner part of the plate.

- A batter who swings up, or uppercuts, is vulnerable to high strikes.
- A batter who strides open, or "steps in the bucket," will have trouble with fastballs away and any off-speed pitch.
- Batters who hold the bat in a vertical position tend to be better on low balls than high.
- Batters who hold the bat in a horizontal position tend to be better on high balls than low.
- A batter who pulls your best fastball foul may be set up for something off-speed.
- A batter who puts a good swing on your best curve was probably looking for something off-speed and may be vulnerable to a fastball.

None of these "rules" is foolproof, of course, but it pays to observe the hitter closely. Anything you can learn will be helpful.

A batter who uses a closed stance (left) is susceptible to hard pitches thrown inside. A batter who holds his bat straight up and down (right) often has difficulty handling low strikes.

Pitch Selection

Deciding which pitch to throw and where to throw it is the essence of pitching. Rule number one is this: don't over-think things. Generally speaking, you should go with your best pitch to your best location. Attack the strike zone. Remember that except in very specific circumstances where you need a strikeout, you want the batter to make contact. What pitch does every batter want to hit? The fastball. Use your fastball and you'll get the batter to swing.

In certain situations you must give extra thought to your pitch selection. For example, if you have two outs, a runner on second base, and a very good hitter at the plate, you should be cautious. The open base (at first) provides you with an opportunity to pitch very carefully to the batter without hurting yourself. Check the on-deck circle to see who is coming up next. There may be a chance to avoid giving the tough batter at the plate anything good to hit. Discretion is the better part of valor. Know which batters in the opposing lineup to avoid when the situation allows it.

114

WELCOME CONTACT

Because young players rarely provide flawless defense, the young pitcher is often guilty of not wanting the batter to put the ball into play. Too many youngsters pitch only for strikeouts. This is wrong. Your job is to make the batter put the ball into play. In major league baseball, 65 percent of all balls hit fair are outs! Learn to covet contact. It keeps your pitch count low and the fielders alert. Also, pay attention when your team takes batting practice. Notice how many of the balls hit in batting practice would be outs in the game. Make them hit it; it's the quickest way to an out.

As a pitcher, you should covet contact. In major league baseball, 65 percent of all balls hit fair are outs!

115

Working with the Umpire

You should also pay attention to how the umpire is calling the game. He, not you, makes the ultimate decision as to whether a pitch is a strike or ball. If he'll call strikes on pitches just wide of the corners, then throw the ball there. Anytime you can get a strike on a pitch that isn't exposed to the strike zone, then that's a pitch you want to throw. If the umpire won't give you the pitch that you're used to getting, then make an adjustment. Also, be careful

> *The best pitch you can throw is a comfortable pitch, the pitch that you believe in, even if it's the wrong pitch.*
>
> —Greg Maddux, major league pitcher

about how you react to a borderline pitch that the umpire calls a ball. If you accept his call with grace, you may get that pitch later in the game. Umpires are like anyone else; they want to (and should) be treated with respect.

Handling Adversity

Almost inevitably, you will find yourself in trouble at some point in the game. The game is almost always decided by how well the pitcher performs when there are runners on base. There are many things you can do to better handle the tough situations in the game. First, you should slow down. This gives you time to think your way through the situation. You need time to engage your brain and figure out what needs to be done and how to do it. Take a deep breath and visualize how you escaped from such a jam before. Focus on the task at hand and not on how you got into the mess. Taking your time also slows down the opposition. It takes away the pace of their rally.

116

Next, realize that the trouble is never quite as bad as you think. In fact, you are always *one pitch away* from everything changing dramatically for the better. Suppose you are facing a bases-loaded, no-outs situation. This is the pitcher's nightmare scenario, right? Not if you apply the correct "one pitch away" thinking.

If you make a good pitch and the batter hits a ground ball, you have an opportunity for a double play. Perhaps he hits a routine infield pop-up, or maybe you make a great pitch to record a strike-out. Suddenly the task of getting out of the inning unscathed

Whether you threw a great pitch or the worst pitch in history, the only thing that really matters is your next pitch.

—Greg Maddux, major league pitcher

doesn't seem so daunting anymore. If your coach didn't think you could make one good pitch, he wouldn't have left you on the mound. Remember: one pitch away.

Picking Up Your Teammates

I've watched young pitchers implode immediately following an error by a teammate. The pitcher becomes so upset at losing an out that he loses his concentration and things go from bad to worse. This doesn't have to be. Instead, follow every error with a heightened sense of concentration, a commitment to not allowing that runner to score.

You are going to "pick up" your teammate by retiring the next batter. Errors are part of the game. No one wants to make an error any more than you want to walk a batter or allow a hit. Make it a practice to tell your teammate, "That's all right, I'll take care of this." Your teammates will have great respect for you, and they will do anything to make a play for you or to get the key hit that helps you win the game.

117

LEAVE YOUR BAT IN THE DUGOUT

As a young pitcher, you may also be a very good hitter, perhaps the best on your team. Your at-bats are often inextricably linked to team success. Nevertheless, you must be able to separate your roles as pitcher and hitter. You cannot let failure at the plate affect your performance on the mound. Once you put down your helmet and bat and pick up your glove and cap, you are a *pitcher*. I have seen too many young pitchers fall apart on the mound following a bad at-bat. Pitching requires complete focus. You can't make good pitches when your mind is still in the batter's box.

Making Adjustments During the Game

Not every pitch or every at-bat or every inning or every game is going to go exactly the way you planned. You are a human being and you will make mistakes. That's why you must have a Plan B, an alternative way of attacking the opposition. Sometimes, though, your problems stem from a breakdown of your mechanics. Obviously, it would be best if you addressed any mechanical flaws with your coach while you're practicing in the bullpen. But you need to be able to correct problems in your mechanics during the game, before things get out of hand. The best pitchers understand their mechanics well enough to be able to diagnose a problem and fix it on the spot—before the coach removes them from the game.

118

The symptoms. Before you can diagnose what's wrong with your mechanics, you must be observant enough to notice the symptoms. Where are your pitches missing? Is there a common pattern? Does your curveball lack its normal sharp break? What does your finish position look like? Is it quite different from when you are throwing well? Once you've identified the symptoms of your problem, you can set about fixing it.

YOU'RE ONLY HUMAN

Some nonstrikes are caused by the frailties of human error. You simply miss your release point early or late, or the pitch barely misses the strike zone. Don't worry about these pitches. You will never become so accomplished as to only throw strikes. Understand that it is inevitable that you will throw many balls during the game. Know the difference between a good ball and a bad ball. Don't try to fix something that isn't broken; the cure can be worse than the disease.

Even if you're having a tough game at the plate (hitting), be sure to stay focused on the task at hand on the pitcher's mound.

Problem	Causes	Remedy
Missing high to your arm side (to the right for a right-handed pitcher)	• You are rushing forward with your upper body, causing your arm to drag and your hand to be under the ball. • You are prematurely opening your lead shoulder, causing your arm to drag and your hand to be under the ball. • You are dropping your throwing elbow below shoulder level, making it difficult to keep your fingers behind and on top of the ball.	Lead to the target with the lower half of your body, keeping your upper body back (and tall), your elbow at shoulder height, and your lead shoulder closed until after your glide foot lands.
Missing low, often in the dirt	• Your glide step is too short, causing your fingers to be too much on top of the ball and your release point to be late. • Your grip is too tight, causing the ball to stick in your hand beyond your ideal release point.	Make sure that your glide step is nearly as long as you are tall (you can check for your footprint in the dirt), and relax your grip on the ball so that your fingers, hand, and wrist have no tension.
Missing away from your arm side (to the left for a right-handed pitcher)	• Your initial alignment is bad. For example, if your lead shoulder (right-handed pitcher) is aligned to the left, you may continue to move left, causing your aiming point to be to the left of the intended target line. • You have a fear of hitting a same-handed batter.	Make certain that your initial alignment to the target line is correct, and understand that pitching close to the batter is part of the game, that it is his responsibility to move away from any close pitch.

The diagnosis and remedy. Now that you've identified a recurring problem, you must identify the cause. The chart on the previous page includes a few of the most common "miss" patterns, the possible causes, and the remedy. Commit this chart to memory and you'll be able to fix a problem before it's too late.

Postgame Evaluation

After the game is over, it is time for you to evaluate your performance. This will help you to develop a plan for continued improvement. Make note of what went well and what needs to get better. Here are some items to consider during your assessment:

If your pitches are repeatedly sailing up and in, perhaps you're rushing to the plate, opening your front shoulder prematurely, or dropping your elbow below your throwing shoulder.

- *Strike-to-ball ratio.* You should have at least 60 percent strikes.
- *First-pitch strikes.* How many times did you throw the first pitch for a strike? Strive for 70 percent.
- *Off-speed pitches for a strike.* Your target is at least 60 percent.
- *First out of the inning.* How many times did you retire the first batter? You want to accomplish this at least two-thirds of the time.
- *Facing opposite-hand hitters.* If you are a right-handed pitcher, how did you do against left-handed batters?
- *Facing the middle of the lineup.* How did you do against the 3-4-5 part of the opposing lineup? These are the batters who can hurt you. Getting them out is often the difference between winning and losing.
- *Frame of mind.* Did you remain focused throughout the game? Did you work fast and attack the strike zone? Did you remain calm in the face of adversity? Assess your mental performance.
- *Mechanics checklist.* Did you notice any breakdown in your mechanics? Is there some part of your delivery that is causing you a problem?

Having someone chart your pitches during the game will make the postgame evaluation much easier. Pitching charts are available through most baseball merchandise catalogs.

Finally, you need to ask yourself and your coach the following question after every game: What can I do to get better? Wanting to get better is the first step toward getting better.

7

FIELDING YOUR POSITION

Your primary responsibility as a pitcher is to throw the ball over the plate. As soon as you do that, you immediately become a fielder. Being a good-fielding pitcher will get you more outs and more wins. That should be all the incentive you need to become a good "glove man" on the mound.

The pitcher is the centerpiece of the defense. Consider these facts:

- The pitcher plugs the biggest hole in the infield.
- A good-fielding pitcher takes away the bunt from the opposition's offensive game plan.
- The pitcher initiates many double plays.
- The pitcher becomes the first baseman on certain ground balls to the right side of the field.
- The pitcher fields some infield pop-ups and directs traffic on others.
- The pitcher backs up bases on throws from the outfield (he is the last line of defense).
- The pitcher covers home on passed balls and wild pitches with a runner on third.
- The pitcher participates in many rundown plays.
- The pitcher provides strikeouts and weak contact that make things easy for the rest of the defense.

Anticipation, Observation, and Communication

The first key to being a good defensive player is to anticipate what's going to happen before it does. The first thing that you should anticipate is that the ball is going to be hit to you. The second thing is to anticipate what you'll do with the ball once you catch it. By predetermining your future actions, you'll be able to act swiftly and decisively once you field the ball.

If you are not directly involved in a play, you should observe the runners and make a decision about who should field the ball, where it should be thrown, and where you should position yourself.

Communication is another key element in good fielding. Communication takes place before and during the play. For example, with a runner on first and less than two outs, you must communicate before the pitch with your middle infielders regarding who will be covering second base if a ground ball is hit to you. An example of communication during the play is when your catcher is fielding

To field your position effectively, you must follow through on every pitch.

a bunt. Since he has his head down to field the ball, you must become his "eyes." Yell in a loud, clear voice telling him to which base to throw the ball, or in some cases, to not throw the ball at all.

The bottom line is that as the pitcher you must be the leader of the defense, both before and after you throw the ball. Those are your outs, so you must be an active participant who uses his brain, his eyes, his mouth, and his glove just as much as his arm.

Fielding Ground Balls and Line Drives

As the fielder (in fair territory) closest to the batter, the pitcher has the least amount of time available to react to a ball hit at him. You must finish in a position that allows you to defend yourself and your position or you'll give up plenty of unnecessary hits, and you'll get

Lend your teammates a helping hand by communicating with them on each play.

a few bruises along the way, too. Make sure that as your back leg hits the ground you are ready:

- You are on the balls of your feet.
- Your weight is evenly balanced.
- Your glove is up and open.
- Your eyes are up and directed toward the hitting zone.

The good news about being the fielder closest to the batter is that if you catch the ball, you have plenty of time to throw the batter or runner out.

Ground Ball with the Bases Empty

The "comebacker" is the ball hit right back at you. If you can catch the ball cleanly, do so. If not, try to knock it down with your glove or your body. Remember, you'll have plenty of time to throw the runner out, because he'll have hardly left the batter's box by the time the ball reaches you. And there isn't any runner, no matter how fast, who can outrun the ball. One caveat: don't try to knock the ball down with your bare hand. One out isn't worth risking serious injury. Use your glove or your body to knock down a ground ball, but never your throwing hand. Once you've fielded the ball, square your shoulders to the target, step directly at the target, and throw the ball crisply with a good follow-through.

127

Ground Ball with Runners on Base

When there are runners on base, you must know to which base you're going to throw when you field a ground ball. This is especially important when the double play is called for. First, communicate with your fielders. Tell them exactly what you plan to do when you field the ball. Where you should throw it depends upon the situation. In all the following situations, assume that there are less than two outs.

Runner on First

Ideally you want to throw the ball to second base to get the lead runner, the beginning of a double play. Most of the time it will be the shortstop covering second base. Square your shoulders, step to the target, and throw the ball chest-high and *over the base*. Do not attempt to lead the fielder to the base! Trust that he'll do his job and get to the base. The only times you should throw to first base in this situation is if the ball is slowly hit to your left or right, or if you bobble the ball, or if you're protecting a big lead and want to make sure of an easy out.

Runners on First and Second

Again, you should get the force-out at second and hope for the double play. The pitcher to shortstop to first (1-6-3) double play is much

DON'T BE A HERO

If you are unfortunate enough to be struck by a line drive or hard ground ball, be realistic about whether or not to continue pitching in that game. Any injury that causes you to change the mechanics of your delivery is serious enough that you should be removed from the game. Altering your mechanics could cause you to injure your arm. Also, changing your mechanics could become a hard habit to break.

Get your injury treated and don't attempt to pitch again until your body allows you to use the good mechanics that made you an effective pitcher in the first place. All coaches love tough pitchers, guys who want to stay in the game, no matter what. But when it comes to your mechanics, discretion is the better part of valor.

With a force at second base, check with your shortstop and second baseman to see who is covering the base on a ball hit back to the pitcher. Make sure this is decided before the pitch.

easier to turn than throwing the ball to the third baseman, because he has to throw the ball all the way across the diamond. You should throw to third base only on a slowly hit ball to the third base side of the mound, or if you bobble the ball and have no time to get a double play. Go to first base only on a slowly hit ball to the right side of the mound. Listen for instructions from your catcher as you field the ball. He can see everything developing directly in front of him.

Runners on First and Third

Unless the runner on third represents the tying or go-ahead run late in the game, you should throw the ball to second base to attempt the double play. If the runner at third is the tying or winning run, you should check him back to the base before throwing the ball to second. (If he breaks for home, throw the ball to the catcher.) This

With the bases loaded, get the force-out at home plate if the ball is hit back to you. Step to the target and throw a chest-high strike to the catcher.

is the most complicated situation you'll face. You should frequently practice defending against the first-and-third situation.

Bases Loaded

At higher levels of baseball, coaches prefer that the pitcher throw the ball to second base in this situation. For young players, though, the pitcher should initiate the double play by throwing the ball to the catcher. Throw the ball chest-high and out over the plate, leading the catcher into fair territory. Make sure of your throw, because you want to cut off the run. If the ball is slowly hit, you may still have time to get the force-out at the plate. Always look for an opportunity to stop a run from scoring.

Runner on Second and/or Third

The force play is not available. Think ahead about how you will handle this situation. As soon as you field the ball, check the position of the runner. If he breaks for the next base, throw him out. If you catch him halfway between the bases, run directly at him, forcing him to run one way or the other. Once he commits to a base, throw the ball to your fielder, then follow the throw and be prepared to be involved in a rundown play. If the runner heads back to his original base, simply throw the ball to first base and take the easy out.

Ground Ball to the Right Side of the Infield

On any ground ball hit to the right side of the infield, you should break toward first base, preparing to cover the base if needed. This play is practiced over and over in preseason and during the season. As soon as the ball is hit, the catcher and all the players in the dugout should shout at you to "get over!" Here are the steps to follow for covering first base:

131

1. React immediately toward first base, no matter how routine the ground ball may seem. (First basemen have been known to bobble routine grounders.)
2. Sprint toward the foul line to a spot about 10 feet short of the base.
3. Slow down and come under control as you reach the foul line.
4. Present a target with your glove and ask for the ball.
5. Catch the ball first; then look for the base.
6. Touch the inside of the base with your right foot and allow your momentum to carry you in toward fair territory. (Touching the base with your left foot or crossing the foul line may get you barreled over by the runner.)

7. Turn back toward the infield to check the position of any base runners.

If you get to the base before receiving the throw, set up like a first baseman, with your foot in contact with the inside of the base. Always yield to the first baseman any time he waves you away from the bag (to receive a throw) or says that he'll take the ball to the base himself.

On ground balls hit to the right side of the infield, immediately break toward first base. Run toward the inside of the base, find it with your right foot, and catch the toss from the first baseman. As you make the catch, push off the base toward the infield to avoid a collision with the base runner.

Fielding Bunts

Bunting is very popular among young hitters. You must know your responsibilities for defending against the bunt. Anticipate the bunt—expect it—and know what you're going to do once you field the ball.

Bases Empty

Get to the ball as quickly as possible. If the ball is still rolling, use your glove. If the ball has come to rest, use your bare hand. Use quick footwork to square your shoulders to first base and use your quickest release. Don't worry too much about the velocity of your throw. A quick, accurate throw is much more important. Also, don't rush your throw, because you probably have more time than you think.

Runner on First

Unless the ball is bunted hard and right at you, your best play will be to first base. Get the sure out. A hitter who is attempting a sacrifice bunt is offering you an out. Take it!

Runners on First and Second

Again, unless the ball is bunted hard to you, your best play is probably to first base. If you are a right-handed pitcher and want to make the play at third base, execute a reverse pivot before throwing. That is, you should field the ball, step away from third base with your right foot, turn your left shoulder and left foot toward third base, and throw the ball.

Squeeze Play

With a runner on third base, less than two outs, and no force play available at the plate, you should be ready for the "squeeze play," a sacrifice bunt designed to drive home a run. If the play is well disguised, you probably won't have a chance to get the runner at home.

If a bunted ball comes to rest, field the ball with your hand. Push off your rear leg to step to first base and make a strong throw.

When the catcher fields the ball, call out where he should direct his throw.

HOLD PROGRAM

Little League pitchers don't need to hold runners on base, because there's no leading allowed while the pitcher is holding the ball. Still, it won't be long before you are charged with the responsibility of holding runners close, so now is not a bad time to start learning the crucial elements of the Hold Program, a system for keeping runners from stealing you blind.

There are many reasons for keeping base runners honest:

- Keeps the double play in order
- Keeps runners out of scoring position
- Gives your catcher a chance to throw out base stealers
- Makes the other team get more hits to score runs
- Takes pressure off your defense

The Hold Program is composed of several simple and logical concepts. Your skill at holding runners close is a product of your commitment. If you accept your responsibility for holding runners, you'll be good at it. If you don't, you won't. Here is a checklist of practices you should incorporate into your Hold Program:

137

- ☐ *Vary the length of time that you hold the ball in the set position.* This makes it difficult for the runner to time your move to the plate.
- ☐ *Learn and use a slide-step delivery.* This abbreviated delivery—minus the normal leg raise—allows you to deliver the ball to the catcher more quickly.
- ☐ *Perfect your pickoff move to first.* A quick and/or deceptive move will force the base runner to take a shorter primary lead, meaning that he'll have to run farther to steal a base.
- ☐ *Hold the ball.* Nothing destroys the rhythm and timing of a base stealer more than a pitcher who holds the ball for long periods of time. The runner will be flat-footed and tense, and he may even break for second before you release the ball, thus giving you an easy out.

Simply throw the ball to first base and get the out. If, however, the batter prematurely squares to bunt, you should pitch the ball high and away from the batter, to make it difficult for him to bunt.

Pop-Ups

In professional baseball the pitcher rarely fields a pop-up. That's partly because he is surrounded by a complement of outstanding fielders. In Little League baseball the pitcher is often the best athlete on the field, so he should field any pop-up he can easily catch. Call for the ball loudly and clearly: "I got it. I got it."

When you can't field the ball, you should bark out instructions as to who should catch the ball: "Tommy! Tommy! Tommy!" Cover the base left vacant by the fielder who is fielding the pop-up. On pop-ups behind the catcher, point to the ball and shout instructions to the catcher: "Straight back!"

Backing Up Bases

Inevitably there will be balls hit to the outfield with runners on base. When this happens, don't just stand there like a statue, lamenting the location of the pitch or the poor pursuit angle taken by your right fielder. I've seen too many pitchers get caught up in the moment, standing behind the mound with their hands on their hips when they should be getting into better position to help their defense. Like it or not, backing up bases is a crucial part of your job. Keep the following in mind:

- Never stand still. There is a place for you to be after every ball hit to the outfield. Get there as quickly as possible.
- Watch the runners as they move around the bases, and react to where the ball is going. On a base hit to the outfield, head for the base that is two bases ahead of the lead runner.

If the ball is popped up to the pitcher's mound, call for the ball and make the catch. When it's popped up to a position player, call out the name of your teammate who should make the catch.

- When you back up a base, stand as far back from the base as the field layout allows. This gives you time to react to an off-line throw. Also, try to place yourself in a direct line with the base and the position of the fielder who is throwing the ball.
- Expect the unexpected. Be prepared for a good throw to be mishandled or to carom off the runner.
- If you catch an overthrow, be prepared to make a play.

On a ball hit to the outfield fence with no runners on base, you should immediately back up third. You're conceding that any ball hit that far is at least a double, so you go to the next base.

Rundowns

The pitcher most often becomes involved in a rundown play after fielding a ball and making the first throw. For example, suppose you field a ground ball and trap the runner between third base and home. You run at the runner and he breaks toward home, so you throw the ball to the catcher and run behind him to cover home. The catcher chases the runner back toward third and gives up the ball too soon. Now you'll have to get involved by receiving a throw from the third baseman.

> *There is always a spot for the pitcher to be. He should never be standing on the mound watching the game go by. The pitcher should always be anticipating where an overthrow might be and pay attention to what the base runners are doing.*
>
> *—Jim Kaat, major league pitcher (16-time Gold Glove winner)*

Backing up bases is an important job. It can stop a team from advancing an extra base or even scoring a run. Make sure you stand back far enough to have time to react to an errant throw.

Receiving the Ball During a Rundown Play

There are three important rules for receiving the ball in a rundown play:

- Go to the same side of the baseline as your teammate and give him a target. You don't want your teammate to have to throw the ball across the path of the runner, and you don't want to get in the way of the runner and subject yourself to an interference call.
- Close ground between yourself and the runner. You want to be able to receive the throw and quickly apply a tag.
- Whenever possible, catch the ball and cover it with your throwing hand while applying the tag. This will keep the ball from being jarred loose by contact. As you apply the tag, quickly step away or disengage yourself from the runner so that you are prepared to make a play on any other runner.

Throwing the Ball During a Rundown Play

There are some simple guidelines for throwing the ball during a rundown:

- Hold the ball high in your throwing hand so that it's easy for your teammate to see.
- Don't fake a throw. Hold the ball high and get the runner moving quickly toward your teammate.
- Don't throw the ball across the path of the runner. Get on the same side of the baseline as your teammate.
- Try to make only one throw to retire the runner. Throw the ball no lower than waist-high and no higher than chest-high.
- When you are chasing a runner back to a base already occupied, do not throw the ball. Tag both runners. The runner advancing to that base will be called out.

In a rundown, try to force the base runner back to his original base.

Fielding Drills

Here are some of the most common fielding drills for pitchers. They all come under the broad heading of Pitcher's Fielding Practice, or PFP.

Comebackers

In this simple drill, the pitcher simulates the delivery of a pitch, then fields a ground ball hit to him by the coach. The pitcher fields the ball and throws to a designated base. You can make the drill more fun by playing a game called "Knockout." In Knockout, the pitcher must field the ball cleanly and make an accurate throw, or he is out of the game. The last pitcher in the game is the winner.

A game of Knockout is a fun and competitive way to work on come-backers. The coach hits balls to one pitcher at a time. The pitcher must field the ball cleanly and make an accurate throw to first base to remain in the game. If he bobbles or throws the ball wild, he's knocked out of the game. Last man standing wins!

Bunts

Combine bunting practice for the hitters with bunt-fielding practice for the pitchers. Wait until the pitcher nearly reaches the ball before calling out a designated base for him to throw to. You may more closely simulate game conditions by not allowing the pitcher to break for the ball until he hears a verbal signal from a coach.

Pop-Fly Priorities

Using a tennis racket and ball, generate pop-ups all over the infield. Teach the pitcher to become a traffic cop by either calling for the ball himself or verbally designating which fielder should catch the ball.

Rundowns

Simulate a rundown between third base and home. The pitcher begins with the ball at home plate and the runner halfway up the baseline. Create a game in which two-man teams (pitcher and infielder) compete to retire the runner with the least number of throws possible. Each team gets four or five attempts, with a point awarded for each time they record an out with only one throw and a point subtracted for each time they allow the runner to be safe.

Covering First

The pitcher simulates a pitch, the coach hits a ground ball to the right side of the infield, and the pitcher covers first. Repeat ten times for each pitcher.

8

CONDITIONING

You won't become the best pitcher you can be unless you commit to a physical conditioning plan. To meet the rigorous demands of the position, you need to develop a flexible, strong, and durable body. You want to remain healthy and to be on the mound in the last inning to finish what you started. There are no shortcuts. You have to work at it. Your program should have three elements: stretching, running (long distance, intervals, sprints), and throwing.

Stretching

You must continually stretch all the muscles in your body. Stretching will make you more flexible, which is in itself a good thing, and it also helps prevent injury. Never stretch cold muscles. Always perform a short, light jog before stretching, so that your muscles are warm. Hold each stretch position for five to ten seconds. Don't bounce up and down during the exercise.

Legs

Begin with your legs, your foundation, and work your way up to the rest of your body. You need strong legs to provide the base over which your upper body functions when throwing the ball.

V stretch. Sit with your legs extended in a V position. Turn your upper body to the right and grab your right ankle. Bend your head and chest toward your knee. Repeat this exercise to the left, and then face forward and bend at the waist and bring your head and chest as close as possible to the ground between your legs.

Hamstrings. Stand straight with your right foot crossed over your left. Bend forward at the waist as far as you can. Repeat the exercise with your left foot crossed over your right.

Butterfly groin stretch. Sit with your legs extended in a V position. Bend your knees so that you can bring the soles of your shoes together. Pull your feet in as close to your groin as possible. Place your elbows against the insides of your knees. Now press your elbows against your knees until you feel your groin stretch.

V stretch

Hamstring stretch

Butterfly groin stretch

Calf stretch   Quadriceps stretch

Calf. Stand facing a wall about three feet away. Place both your hands against the wall at about shoulder height and lean forward. Bring your right foot forward, keeping your left leg straight with your left foot remaining flat on the ground. Start moving your left leg as far away from the wall as you can while keeping your back straight and your left heel flat on the ground. Repeat the exercise by switching legs.

Quadriceps. Stand on your right leg. Bend your left leg behind you and grab your left foot. Pull your left foot up and in toward you. Repeat the exercise by switching legs.

Back

You'll need a strong, flexible back to be a starting pitcher. The pitching delivery requires you to powerfully rotate the core of your body on every pitch, and your back plays a big role in that movement.

Stretching the lower back

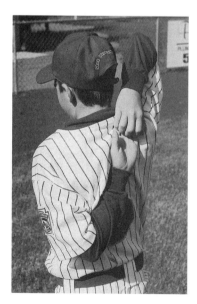

Shake-hands
stretch

Lower back and abdominals. Sit with your right leg extended, your left knee flexed, and your left foot on the outside of your right knee. Place your right elbow inside your left knee and turn your upper body to the left as far as possible. Use your left arm behind you to keep your balance. Repeat the exercise by switching legs.

Crossover stretch. Stand with your feet more than shoulder-width apart. Lift both arms straight over your head. Bend forward at the waist and attempt to touch the ground to the outside of your right foot with your left hand. Repeat by switching sides.

Shake hands. Hold your left arm down at your side and lift your right arm straight above your head. Bend your right arm so that your right hand is behind your back. Bend your left arm up so that your left hand is between your shoulder blades. Now clasp hands and pull up with your right hand and down with your left. Repeat by switching hand positions. If you can't clasp hands behind your back, use a towel that you can grab with each hand. Pull on the towel with both hands to get your stretch.

> *Before I do anything, I have an entire stretching routine that I go through. I don't touch a ball until I'm properly stretched.*
> —Curt Schilling, major league pitcher

153

Shoulders

The shoulder is one area of your body that takes an incredible beating from the act of pitching a baseball. It's also one of the most under-trained parts of your body. You must pay particular attention to keeping your shoulder muscles flexible and strong.

Pull (behind). Lift your right arm above your head and bend your

Pull behind shoulder stretch

Pull across shoulder stretch

elbow so that your right hand is behind your right shoulder. Place your left hand on the back of your upper right arm (near the elbow) and pull your arm toward your head. You should feel your shoulder being stretched. Repeat by switching sides.

Pull (front). Hold your right arm at shoulder level and in front of you so that it is parallel to the ground. Place your left hand on your right elbow and pull your arm in and to the left. You should feel your shoulder muscles being stretched. Repeat by switching sides.

Wrist and Forearm

Your wrist and forearm play a big role as you release a pitch. You want them to be loose (flexible) so that you get maximum snap on each delivery.

Forearm stretch (pull up)

Forearm stretch (pull down)

Wrist down. Hold your right arm straight out in front of you with your hand palm down. Hold your right hand down (with your left hand) with your wrist fully flexed and hold it for ten seconds. Repeat by switching sides.

Wrist up. Hold your right arm straight out in front of you with your hand palm down. Hold your right hand up (with your left hand) with your wrist fully flexed and hold it for ten seconds. Repeat by switching sides.

Running

When your legs get tired, your mechanics become flawed. It's that simple. You can't pitch, at least not for long, if you don't have strong, durable legs. Remember, your legs are the foundation over which your upper body functions. Any structure, whether it's a building or the human body, is only as strong as its foundation. You want strong legs for those late innings when the game is on the line. If you want to finish what you started, you should develop a running program that strengthens your legs. Your running program will have three parts: distance, intervals, and sprints.

Distance

Baseball people refer to this part of the running program as "LSD," or long slow distance. As a young pitcher, you should establish a reasonable goal for how far and how long you can jog. I recommend that you attempt to run for no more than ten or fifteen minutes, or about a mile. As you get older, you can lengthen your jogs to two to five miles, depending on your cardiovascular fitness. You should do your long-distance run twice a week, and it should be the only running you do on those days.

Running sprints with teammates can make an unpopular exercise more enjoyable.

Intervals

Interval running is when you alternate between slow jogging and sprinting. Most pitchers do this by jogging from one foul pole across the outfield to the other foul pole and then sprinting back. Because you are a young pitcher, you must be reasonable about the pace at which you can run intervals and about how many you can run. When you first begin interval training, try to go back and forth between foul poles three to five times. Do this three times per week. As you gain endurance, you should increase the length of your interval workout. The best time to "run poles" is immediately after practice.

Sprinting

Sprinting is useful because it will help you with those quick bursts of power that you need when pitching a baseball. Begin with 30-yard sprints and extend to 40 or 50 yards as you gain strength and endurance. Allow yourself some time between sprints for recovery. You should get some sprint work in nearly every day after practice.

Running isn't easy. It requires a commitment to getting better. And it requires mental toughness to run on hot, humid summer days. If you are tough enough to run when others won't, you'll get a bonus beyond physical fitness: you'll feel better about yourself. You'll feel special, because you're training when others aren't. If you can tough it out in training, you can tough it out on the mound. A rigorous conditioning program will tell you a lot about yourself.

Throwing Program

Chapter 1 described an in-season throwing program for young pitchers. Use this as a sample representation of the least you should be doing. How much more you can do is an individual thing. The bottom line is this: unless you are injured, you should be doing some form of throwing every day. Mix it up between soft tossing (playing catch), bullpen work (at something less than maximum exertion), long tossing, and game pitching. Arm troubles and under-developed arm strength and endurance are mostly products of too little throwing, not too much. Don't baby your arm.

Off-Season Throwing

Young athletes should be balanced. Play as many sports as you can. If you can find some time during the off-season to throw the base-ball, then by all means go ahead. But be sure that your off-season throwing program isn't too rigorous; you're too young to be going full blast all year. Confine yourself to once or twice a week. Your arm needs a break once in a while, whether you're a Little League pitcher or a major league pitcher.

Arm Care and Maintenance

Muscle soreness is a part of every pitcher's life, and you'll be no different. Pitching a baseball in a game is a tearing-down process.

Strong abdominal muscles add velocity to your pitches and improve endurance. Sit-ups are an excellent exercise for strengthening the abdominal muscles.

You need to behave wisely after the game so that your arm recovers quickly. Ice your arm after the game and talk to your doctor about whether you should take an over-the-counter anti-inflammatory after pitching. Icing your arm isn't fun. But neither is missing your next start because you didn't take proper care of your arm after the last start. Just do it!

Push-ups can be used to warm up the body before heading down to the bullpen. They also help build upper-body strength.

Weight Training

Weight training should not be part of your conditioning program. *Little League pitchers are too young to be lifting weights.* I know that some of you will do it anyway. If you do train with weights, consult with a physical trainer before starting. Use nothing more than light dumbbells (one or two pounds).

Index